ACROSS THE
CURRICULUM

Hilary A. Radnor

CASSELL

Cassell
Villiers House, 41/47 Strand, London WC2N 5JE
387 Park Avenue South, New York, NY 10016–8810

First published 1994

British Library Cataloguing-in-Publication Data
A catalogue record for this book is available from the British Library.

Library of Congress Cataloging-in-Publication Data

Radnor, Hilary.
Across the curriculum / Hilary Radnor.
p.   cm.—(Education matters)
Includes bibliographical references and index.
ISBN 0–304–32832–4
1. Interdisciplinary approach in education—England.
2. Interdisciplinary approach in education—Wales.   I. Title.
II. Series.
LB1564.G7R33   1994
375′.00942—dc20   93–42673
                                         CIP

ISBN 0–304–32832–4 (hardback)
0–304–32834–0 (paperback)

Phototypeset by Intype, London
Printed and bound in Great Britain by
Biddles Ltd, Guildford and King's Lynn

EDUCATION MATTERS

General Editor: Ted Wragg

ACROSS THE CURRICULUM

WITHDRAWN

CONTENTS

FOREWORD

Professor E. C. Wragg, Exeter University

During the 1980s a succession of Education Acts changed considerably the nature of schools and their relationships with the outside world. Parents in particular were given more rights and responsibilities, including the opportunity to serve on the governing body of their child's school. The 1988 Education Reform Act in particular, by introducing for the first time a National Curriculum, the testing of children at the ages of 7, 11, 14 and 16, local management, including financial responsibility and the creation of new types of school, was a radical break with the past.

In the wake of such rapid and substantial changes it was not just parents and lay people, but also teachers and other professionals working in education, who found themselves struggling to keep up with what these many changes meant and how to get the best out of them. The *Education Matters* series addresses directly the major topics of reform, such as the new curriculum, testing and assessment, the role of parents and the handling of school finances, considering their effects on both primary and secondary education.

The aim of the series is to present information about the challenges facing education in the remainder of the twentieth century in an authoritative but readable form. The books in the series, therefore, are of particular interest to parents, governors and all those interested in education, but are written in such a way as to give an overview of student and experienced teachers or other professionals in the field.

Each book gives an account of the relevant legislation and background, but, more importantly, stresses the practical implications of change with specific examples of what is being or can be done to make reforms work effectively. The authors of each book are not only authorities in their field, but also have direct experience of the matters they write about, and that is why the *Education Matters* series makes an important contribution to both debate and practice.

PREFACE

Throwing babies out with bathwater is a common crime among reformers. Indeed most 'reforms' widely overshoot their target, and have to be dragged back painfully. So it was with the experimenting educators of the 1960s; so it is with the rigorous retrenchers of the 1980s and 1990s.

Educating the whole child was an expensive undertaking, if done well. It was also potentially subversive, encouraging children to question and doubt and to have aspirations beyond the aspirations of their homes, opening windows for them, and letting in wonder, hope and ambition. Part of that process was the bringing together of many learning activities into one unforgettable experience, the experience that makes learning more like turning on a light than climbing a staircase: a light across the curriculum.

The painful and beautiful journey in search of the whole curriculum has ended in a rather dull motel, with its neat compartments equipped with all the useful things one needs in life but a bit short on the living. The freedom of the secret garden was bound to provoke an outcry for more rigour and order, more, heaven forgive us, 'relevance' – relevance being preached by many people of power and influence who have reached their position through the great privilege of an irrelevant education! Now many educators are saying, 'Steady on, we all wanted more coherence and progression in the curriculum, but we didn't want the magic cut up into motel rooms of neat appearance but no inspiration.' The chorus in support of the threatened cross-curricular themes grows louder, and Hilary Radnor adds a powerful voice to the others. The integrated study of the environment, citizenship, health education, drama – all involve the knowledge and skills that belong to discrete areas of learning but all at the same time represent an awakening, a making-the-connection, a recognition of *why* we need to be able to read and add up and observe and measure and compare.

My observation of children – my own and the many I have spent time with – suggests that only a tiny minority can learn and enjoy learning things they cannot see the point of, while for most of them prior knowledge of what they are going to use the knowledge and skills for is needed.

The exploration and justification in this book of the many vital inter-subject connections – the common themes, the unity of many branches of learning in one experience or investigation – is a valuable contribution to the debate. Perhaps the pendulum will soon swing again, given a little encouragement, in favour of that endangered species, the whole curriculum.

Joan Sallis

ACKNOWLEDGEMENTS

I wish to thank all the pupils and teachers in the schools I visited in different parts of England who were happy to share their cross-curricular experiences and ideas with me, with a special thanks to the primary schools mentioned in Chapter 3.

Thanks also to the BA/BSc students at the School of Education, University of Exeter, whose lessons are included: Alison Allen, Jeffrey Anderson, Rebecca Argyle, Elizabeth Bradshaw, Mark Bradshaw, Sabina Butcher, David Carless, Adam Chase, Ricardo Dominiguez, Hazel Goodie, Simon Graydon, Jane Holland-Lloyd, Angela Lee, David Locke, Diane Summers, Craig Sutton, David Weeks and Madeleine Warner. I extend my gratitude to all the students whose research and writing is included in this book and who have been mentioned in the appropriate chapters.

Finally, particular thanks to Westlands School, Torquay, where much of the cross-curricular development work took place with the generous support of the headteacher and staff and skilfully managed with efficiency, tact and humour by the deputy head Mrs Val Thomasson.

Hilary Radnor

Chapter 1

THE CURRICULUM IN OUR SCHOOLS: THE WHOLE CURRICULUM

Schools are the prominent part of contemporary society's formal organization of education. They are particular institutions, separated out from other spheres of social life and invested with the function of socializing young people into the culture of society. As the pace of change has accelerated markedly in the decades since World War II, an increasingly important part of this socializing process is to prepare young people for adult life in this dynamic, ever-changing world.

As society changes so, too, does society's expectations of schools. Schools are inextricably linked to the forces of societal change. State-maintained institutions, dependent on the state for their survival, are subject to the prevailing beliefs and values that drive the economic, political and educational systems by which society is organized. In a democratic society, these beliefs and values alter as new governments are elected with different manifestos. Consequently, the administration and practical functioning of the education system is an on-going and established political activity. Kogan (1978, p. 15) argues that education cannot be divorced from politics, since 'politics are those processes of discourse through which members of society seek to assert and ultimately reconcile their wishes'.

The overriding expectation from education is that it should provide the individual with the means to be successful in the world which she or he inhabits. In other words, educating is about achieving. There is an expectation that the individual wants to achieve in order to succeed in life. The ability of the education system to enable each individual child to achieve

1

success is bound up in the form, structure and conception of the knowledge that makes up the school curriculum. The school curriculum is a social artefact, constituted of those elements of our human understanding and experience that have evolved and developed over time, a selection of our cultural heritage. Exactly what facets (knowledge, skills, understandings, values, way of knowing, etc.) of our cultural heritage are considered suitable and worthwhile to be passed on from generation to generation has been contested, discussed and debated. Therefore, the curriculum can be perceived not only as a selection of our cultural heritage but also as a cultural tool. David Hamilton (1990, p. 38) states that it is 'more likely to reflect the cultural selections, values and aspirations of powerful social groups than the cultural assumptions and aspirations of powerless groups.' What we have now in the National Curriculum is a curriculum framework that may be interpreted as an aggregation of the different beliefs about what is appropriate to teach in schools held by those in a position to influence policy as well as by those in a position to legislate on policy. So, inevitably, some beliefs and values have won over others.

The 1988 Education Reform Act specified ten subjects for the National Curriculum, naming three as core subjects (English, Mathematics and Science) and seven as foundation subjects (History, Geography, Technology, Music, Art, Physical Education and, at secondary level, a foreign language). The terms 'core' and 'foundation' are used, as the Act states that these National Curriculum subjects constitute the basic curriculum, the minimum requirement expected under the law. These subjects would take up 70 to 80 per cent of curriculum time, which implies that the whole curriculum offering in schools is expected to go beyond the teaching of these ten subjects.

The National Curriculum Council (a body set up by the Secretary of State to oversee the implementation of the National Curriculum) in their document, *The Whole Curriculum* (1990a) identify curricular activities which they feel schools need to address when placing the National Curriculum in the context of the whole school. Part of the introduction (p. 1) states this clearly.

> Section 1 of the Education Reform Act 1988 (ERA) places a statutory responsibility upon schools to provide a broad and balanced curriculum which:
>
> • promotes the spiritual, moral, cultural, mental and physical development of pupils at school and of society; and
> • prepares pupils for the opportunities, responsibilities and experiences of adult life.
>
> The National Curriculum alone will not provide the necessary breadth, but the ten subjects together with religious education (defined in the Act as the 'basic curriculum') can form the foundation to be augmented by:
>
> • religious education;
> • additional subjects beyond the ten subjects of the National Curriculum;
> • an accepted range of cross-curricular elements; and
> • extra-curricular activities.

This description shows that, in the context of the National Curriculum, the word 'curriculum' has become virtually synonymous with the word 'subject'. Traditionally, the concept curriculum has had a number of definitions which are worth reiterating. The dictionary definition reads: 'a course to be run', if you look in a dictionary (e.g. the *Concise Oxford*) you will see that the Latin root of curriculum is *currere* (to run). The original course to be run was a chariot race; now, it is a course of study. Modern-day curriculum theorists, definitions are equally inclusive and cite in more detail what a course of study entails. For example, Jenkins and Shipman (1976) state:

> A curriculum is the formulation and implementation of an educational proposal to be taught and learned within the school or other institution and for which that institution accepts responsibility at three levels: its rationale, its actual implementation and its effects.

Another curriculum theorist and developer, Lawrence Stenhouse (1975), put it slightly differently, emphasizing that the curriculum structure set up in the planning stage should be both rigorous and practical. He also stressed, as does the other definition, the importance of the professionals being responsible for their curriculum programmes:

> An attempt to communicate the essential principles and features of an educational proposal in such a form that it is open to critical scrutiny and capable of effective translation into practice.

Present-day practising teachers also have an inclusive conceptualization of curriculum. During an in-service day the following definitions emerged in discussions with the teachers.

> A set of criteria covering all areas of the child's affective, cognitive and psychomotor development which will act as a guideline for teachers during the education of that child.

> Everything that occurs in the school that aids pupil development.

> To provide the pupils with various learning experiences encompassing the major academic subjects as well as those qualities brought out in the ethos of the total school environment, e.g. health education, personal and social education, and careers education and guidance.

It is clear from this variety of definitions that until the appropriation of the term 'curriculum' (by the government and the writers of the Act) to denote the statutory school subjects, the concept of curriculum encompassed all learning experiences that we consciously structured within the school timetable, saving the term 'extra-curricular' to describe the voluntary activities beyond the compulsory school day.

This narrowing of the term, as a label to denote particular subject matter, assumes the primacy of the traditionally established subjects as the way to structure and organize knowledge in order to educate young people. As the National Curriculum permeates the whole education system over the next decade, it will become commonplace to view subjects as the curriculum, and to consider other learning activities and experiences as cross-curricular, meaning across the subjects.

This book is about these learning experiences designated,

through parliamentary decree, as cross-curricular. This chapter in particular looks more closely at what lies behind the NCC description of the school curriculum, and addresses the question of why it has been felt necessary to include the notion of cross-curricular elements. A brief historical sketch of key curriculum ideas and practices that have affected both primary and secondary education in recent times will serve to show the educational significance of the cross-curricular elements. However, to show their relevance in the education of all our young people growing up in a democracy, we need first to go back a little into the history of educational developments and ideas.

From past to present – the making of a curriculum structure

Within our democratic society, the various political parties have guided the direction of the education system through legislation. The overall structure of the system today is the result of a series of Education Acts, dating back to the nineteenth century. Victorian society was a stratified class society and the evolution of schooling reflected this. Each of the classes – the upper, the middle and the lower – had their own type of schools, developed independently of one another, in the belief that each class needed education for distinctly different purposes (Smith 1931, Curtis 1967, Roach 1971). The Education Act of 1870 made attendance at school compulsory, for the first time, for all children up to the age of twelve. It did this by plugging the gaps in the provision of elementary schools in order to bring the working class up to a minimum level of competence; the schools were expected to teach only reading, writing, arithmetic and scripture. However, it made no attempt to link the primary stage of education to the growing number of secondary schools. In effect, the attitude of the times – the rigid class divisions of Victorian society – locked the working classes out of educational progression.

It was not until the twentieth century, and the Education Act of 1902, that the children of all social classes in England and Wales had direct access to secondary education and beyond. This Act created local education authorities (LEAs) empowered to co-ordinate elementary and higher education, thus creating the possibilities for bright young people in the lower classes to continue their education. However, a secondary school education was not a free education; parents had to pay, although the LEAs were permitted to provide scholarships from grants given by central government. The schools received LEA grants only if they offered the pupils a four-year course of a general educational nature, i.e. including English language, one language other than English, mathematics, science and drawing. Also, provision had to be given for manual work and physical exercise and, in girls' schools, for housewifery.

This emphasis on academic subjects endorsed the links that had been established between the élite public schools and the burgeoning middle-class grammar schools and the universities of Oxford and Cambridge in particular. The universities, in controlling their own entrance qualifications, exerted a strong influence on what was taught in schools. Gaining access to the university and thus entering into a world of academic scholarship was considered the desired apex of schooling and education, so it is not surprising that the Regulations for Secondary Schools 1904 set the context for an education favoured by the universities.

The expansion of secondary education acted as spur to the proliferation of examinations, but the Board of Education felt there was a need to rationalize the different examinations on offer, and this led the university examining bodies to modify their schemes and to the emergence in 1917 of the School Certificate for 16-year-olds. The School Certificate was a general examination, academic in nature, and required at least five subjects to be offered, including one from each of three groups: English subjects; foreign languages; and science and mathematics. It rapidly became the concern of the grammar schools and these academic subjects dominated the school curriculum. Even a cursory look, as this is, at the history of the development of schooling in this country, shows the high status given to academic theoretical knowledge taught through school subjects approved by the universities. The evolution of the School Certificate from a group-subject examination to the single-subject O-level examinations in 1951, leading to A-levels and university entrance, served to guarantee the preservation of high-status academic subjects as the core of the school curriculum.

The emergence of the present structure

As a democracy, we in Britain elect our government and invest power in the ruling party to legislate on our education system. The present British government has initiated and implemented far-reaching educational changes, in which curriculum organization and structure have been central. The 1988 Education Act has gone further than any previous education act; it stipulates, in no uncertain terms, the nature of the curriculum to be followed by every 5- to 16-year-old in England and Wales attending a school funded by the state.

Historically, this Act can be seen to have grown out of a dissatisfaction, expressed from the early 1960s onwards, with the educational standards of children attending state schools. At the Association of Education Committees (of the LEAs) conference in 1976, James Hamilton, Permanent Secretary at the Department of Education and Science (DES), reiterating the feeling of David Eccles, the Conservative Minister of Education in the 1960s, said, 'I believe that the so-called secret garden of the curriculum cannot be allowed to remain so secret after all, and that the key to the door must be found and turned, (Devlin and Warnock, 1977, p. 13). This statement heralded the beginning of the recent government involvement in curriculum practices in the nation's schools. In 1976, James Callaghan, the Labour Prime Minister, launched the 'great debate' on education at Ruskin College, with a speech which intimated to teachers and educationalists that there needed to be a greater association between education and the world of work. Education for its own sake was no longer enough; teaching methods and curriculum needed to be reviewed and the teachers had to be more accountable to the public they served.

7

There was a distinct turn away from the softly-softly approach of the Labour Government when the Conservative Party took office in 1979. The period of Margaret Thatcher as Prime Minister set in motion a progression of right-wing reforms that has altered the relationship between the teacher and the general public. A series of government papers, DES documents and HMI reports culminated in the 1988 Education Act and the National Curriculum. So, decisions about which major elements of our cultural heritage are deemed worthy to be handed on to our children are now controlled by law, and are no longer left to the professional educators in schools, colleges and universities. Curriculum structure and content are enshrined in what are called Orders that need parliamentary approval to change.

In Clause 2 of the Act, the stated aim of this curriculum is to prescribe a number of school subjects and specify in relation to each:

- knowledge, skills and understandings which pupils of different abilities and maturities are expected to have;
- matters, skills and processes which are required to be taught to pupils of different abilities and maturities; and
- arrangements for assessing pupils.

Ten subjects were specified in the 1988 Act. Historical precedence seemed to have won through; the same high-status traditional academic subjects featured, correspond in the main to those defined as being central to the education of the nation's children in 1902 and figuring in the School Certificate introduced in 1917.

'Knowing' through the academic subject

What can be seen as a continuity with the past and the power of inherited tradition is the pre-eminence of subject-centred knowledge which is believed to be related primarily to academic (or propositional) knowledge i.e. knowledge that tells you something – theoretical knowledge – facts, concepts, principles and generalizations. This is generally referred to as the academic subject; each academic subject corresponds to and is derived from scholarly university disciplines – the word 'discipline' coming from the Latin verb, *descere* (to learn). Each subject discipline is therefore a package of developed knowledge organized for learning.

The use of disciplines as the content of the curriculum is supported and justified by numerous educational philosophers. Phenix (1962), for example, distinguishes between disciplined and undisciplined knowledge. He states that a discipline is a conceptual system, gathering together a group of concepts into a common framework of ideas with the goal of simplifying understanding and also revealing significant patterns and relationships. It is a living body of knowledge that excites further questions and discovery, with each new idea generated through the disciplined techniques of enquiry growing out of the theories and ideas previously acquired. The student, therefore, is introduced and initiated into a way of knowing and thinking that has stood the test of both time and critical enquiry and which has been selected out as knowledge worth learning.

Hirst (1969) argues for logical structures in the curriculum. He believes that the purpose of education is, for all children, the development of rational thinking, which is acquired through an understanding of the distinctive characteristics of the disciplines. He states (Hirst 1969, p. 150):

> There are thus within knowledge a number of distinct types of rational judgment. From considerations of this kind, it can be seen that the acquisition of knowledge in any area involves the mastery of an inter-related group of concepts, of operations of these, of particular criteria of truth and validity associated with these concepts ...

Hirst suggests that the most rational way in which to develop these distinct modes of understanding would be by direct organization of the curriculum into units corresponding to the ways of knowing, as structured in the academic disciplines. He claims that there is good historical precedence for this as it is precisely what takes place to a large extent in the traditional subjects curriculum of the grammar school.

The core of the school curriculum – mathematics, science and English – and the majority of the foundation subjects – history, geography and foreign languages – are part of the traditional academic subjects, with the school subject drawing from the stock of knowledge within the discipline being maintained, developed, evaluated and commented on at university level. Goodson (1983) defines school subjects as 'pure . . . abstract' . . . a body of knowledge enshrined in syllabuses and textbooks, and as this knowledge is written down, he argues that it is possible to assess, through tests and examinations, exactly what components of the knowledge have been learnt. The children who learn the most achieve the highest marks and hence, through this means, academically bright children are selected out for higher education.

The student becomes the recipient of a selection of the knowledge decided on. As regards the National Curriculum, this knowledge selection is clearly given for each statutory subject issued to every teacher in the state system. The teacher, already knowledgeable through having been initiated when trained in the subject, is the knower with the responsibility of helping the students to make sense of and master this presented knowledge.

The art of teaching school subjects and learning the prescribed knowledge is complex. Hamilton (1990) describes teaching and learning as the unpacking and repacking of a curriculum storehouse; the teacher has to make this storehouse of human experience accessible to the learners and the learners have to be able to find ways of linking what they already know and their experiences to this new knowledge being offered. The traditional way is through the didactic approach, i.e. the teacher tells the student the facts, the way to enquire and so on, and then tests whether the student has 'taken them in' by setting questions and exercises and marking them. There is an emphasis on learning from textbooks, worksheets, and/or videos as well as from the teacher standing at the front of the class and giving information and explaining concepts and principles by using the blackboard – or whiteboard, or overhead projector, depending on how 'technological' the teacher is and the resources available in the school. With the National Curriculum, the subject knowledge has been decided and atomized into particular units. To use Hamilton's analogy, 'the curriculum storehouse' has gatekeepers, with access to some parts of the storehouse strictly controlled and entry allowed only with and authorized person!

Other ways of 'knowing'

Although subject-centred knowledge has a pre-eminent place in the curriculum, there are other ways of knowing that do not depend on transmission of propositional knowledge. These have been seen in learning contexts outside schools – in the home, learning on the job, learning by following the example and copying an expert and so on. In the past, many people did not have schooling, but still they successfully managed their lives by observing what was going on around them, by experimenting and, trying things out, by listening to others and asking questions, by taking risks and working things out for themselves. To summarize for the purposes of our discussion here, these ways of knowing and learning are associated with conceptions of the *productive* – learning the skills of how to do something that is useful to the individual and the community – and the *practical* – learning how to select appropriate knowledge and have the skills to use that knowledge to make choices, to solve the problems inherent in managing successfully in everyday life.

Control over the education system manifests itself in the arguments associated with the place, value and hence the aims of education in our society, with certain beliefs and values having successfully become central to the organization of the school curriculum. As already noted, this is the pre-eminence of subject-centred knowledge taught within the subject frame of reference and particularly emphasizing academic (propositional) knowledge, while the practical and productive modes of learning, though very important in everyday life, traditionally take second place in formal schooling.

However, the writings of many educational philosophers and practitioners actively disagree with this view; they have developed well-founded educational ideas grounded in different beliefs and values about not only what should be taught in schools but also how it should be taught. These ideas take many forms, but in essence, it is argued that to be an educated person – to be able to take control over one's everyday life – involves the interplay of the theoretical, the practical and the productive. This view emphasizes that learning in school should take account of this, and should not just be about acquiring facts and information. Time has to be built into the curriculum to engage in learning strategies which help the learner make sense of that knowledge, incorporating it into an existing meaning and value system, so that the learner can use that knowledge to improve his/her ability to operate in real situations. It is argued that for a broad and balanced education each of the three ways of knowing – the theoretic, the practical and the productive – need to be present.

When we look at the practice in schools today, we can see influences of different educational philosophies, since educational ideas do have an effect on teaching approaches. One of the most influential thinkers was John Dewey (1859–1952), an American whose ideas spread beyond the boundaries of the USA and inspired educational innovators in countries throughout the world. His, grand concept was *experience*, a concept he employed for the purpose of connecting the person as a dynamic biological entity with the person's environment. The mind, or more specifically intelligence, is for Dewey not a fixed substance, and knowledge is not a set of static concepts. Intelligence is the power the person possesses to cope with his/her environment. Thinking is not an individual act carried on in private, in isolation from practical problems; thinking and doing are intimately related.

In *Democracy and Education* John Dewey; (1966, p. 344) promotes a theory of knowledge that embraces the theoretical, the practical and the productive;

Knowledge in its strict sense of something possessed consists of our intellectual resources – of all habits that render our action intelligent. Only that which has been organized into our disposition so as to enable us to adapt the environment to our needs and to adapt our aims and desires to the situation in which we live is really knowledge. Knowledge is not just something which we are now conscious of, but consists of the dispositions we consciously use in understanding what now happens. Knowledge as an act is bringing some of our dispositions to consciousness with a view to straightening out a perplexity, by conceiving the connection between ourselves and the world in which we live.

This view of knowledge, that it results from the creative power of the individual, encourages the notion of school learning a a dynamic process of enquiry and problem-solving. In both primary and secondary education these ideas have found a place.

The primary sector

As primary education evolved from the elementary school of Victorian England with its concentration on reading, writing and arithmetic, advances in psychological theories about the way children learn encouraged different interpretations as to how knowledge ought to be organized in the classroom. The Plowden Report (DES 1967) on primary education endorsed progressive views on education. It encouraged primary teachers to move away from subject knowledge transmitted as discrete units. Instead, they were advised to draw from the cultural stock of knowledge and to organize their teaching in such a way that the child was placed at the centre of the learning process. Then, each child's stage of intellectual development, practical interests and emotional needs were to become the basis for teacher decisions about the curriculum to be taught (DES 1967: part 5, p. 197).

Rigid division of the curriculum into subjects tends to interrupt children's trains of thought and of interest and to hinder them from realizing the common elements in problem solving. These are among the many reasons why some work, at least, should cut across subject divisions at all stages in the primary school.

13

Methodologically, this has meant that the primary practice considered as 'good' since the late 1960s is an educational environment that provides opportunities for integrating knowledge forms across subjects. Topic and project work has evolved that enables the child to become actively engaged in building from previous experience through participating in practical tasks. In primary classrooms across the country this child-centred approach, with active involvement in concrete tasks, exists side by side with more traditional methods. Bennett (1990), in summarizing the research of primary practice in the 1980s, notes that language and mathematics work remained as a central feature of classroom work with a wide variation of style, content and delivery. The fact is that the structure of the primary school, with one teacher assigned to a class and responsible for teaching virtually the whole curriculum offers the kind of environment where integrating across subject divisions is possible and manageable. The teacher can build in flexibility, rearrange the classroom to suit the activity, and make the most of having sole responsibility of the class for the school day, by integrating different subject material or concentrating exclusively on particular aspects of learning for set periods. In the primary classroom, subject-centred studies and integrated topic work can exist together in a balanced way.

The secondary sector

Due to the pre-eminence of the academic subject tradition, it is not surprising that the typical secondary school structure revolves around the subject department. Pupils are taught by specialist teachers trained in the tradition of their subject, who tend to see themselves as part of their own subject community – hence, their strong identification with their subject department. In any secondary school members of a department will be sitting together in the staff room; they will, have a subject or faculty office where they spend their breaks, hold their meetings and prepare their lessons. The organization of secondary school finances also has the subject department as the main reference point – resources are allocated by subject and the head of each department has an allowance to organize and promote their own subject. Coupled with this, is the important end-point at 16 where the external subject examination, the GCSE, takes precedence over all other qualifications in the school. Both teachers and pupils relate to one another, in the main through the subject being taught. The ethos of the secondary school is therefore shaped by the organization, style and effectiveness of the subject areas.

Expecting the student to develop as an intelligent human being through the learning of subject knowledge has proved to be successful – for young people with a certain type of intelligence, generally labelled as having high academic ability. However, this has not been the case for those who fail to make cognitive 'connections' between the knowledge transmitted to them and their own meaning and value systems i.e. those generally labelled as having average or below average academic ability or simply 'less able'.

By the late 1960s, with the increase in understanding about the different modes of learning and alternative ways of organizing knowledge for teaching purposes, many teachers began to question the value of what they were doing – for the majority of students. Curriculum reform resulted in changes to make the curriculum more useful and relevant for the less able; students were encouraged to construct knowledge for themselves and, to become active meaning makers. Much of this happened within subjects, with the emphasis moving from subject perception, as a body of knowledge to be transmitted, to using the subject material as ways of thinking, enquiring and investigating human experience. The ideas inspired by John Dewey – his view of the interrelationship of theory and practice – were influencing the teaching and learning styles in the schools, albeit in a limited sense. Learning was seen as being more than reading and writing, and some classroom practice included peer group discussions, enquiry projects, practical tasks, role-play and simulations.

Nevertheless, these curriculum reforms were not seen to go far enough; young people needed to be trained to cope with the new technological advances in society. There was a growing concern about the relationship between what was being learnt at school and the world of work, which gave rise to the launching of the 'great debate' of the Labour Government in 1975. This debate initiated links between schools and industry, and new courses for 14- to 16-year-olds directly geared to prepare those school-leavers not going into further or higher education.

Locally conceived initiatives gave way to a national initiative introduced by the Conservative Government in 1982: the Technical and Vocational Education Initiative (TVEI). This initiative was well resourced; it was funded by the Department of Employment in order to ensure clear links with the world of industry and commerce. Professor Richard Pring, who has researched and written extensively on TVEI, perceives the initial response by the schools as a reflection of the prevailing culture of secondary education (Pring 1992, p. 5).

> The initial criticism of TVEI depended upon an understanding of liberal education in which sharp contrasts were drawn between a curriculum which 'liberated' through focus upon the 'perfection of the intellect' and a curriculum which emphasised practical modes of learning, utility and relevance. Education (what schools are concerned with) was contrasted with training (what employers take responsibility for); knowledge and understanding were contrasted with skills acquisition; liberal values of intrinsic worth were contrasted with the utilitarian ones of TVEI; intellectual virtues were opposed to the newly arrived commercial virtues of enterprise and entrepreneurship; the autonomy of educational traditions and institutions was opposed to the loss of that autonomy to employers and the Department of Employment.

As TVEI was implemented in schools, teachers tempered the strong vocational and training criteria: the productive mode of learning. As Pring (1992, p. 1–2) informs us:

> To put in a nutshell what happened, the TVEI curriculum liberalised an otherwise narrowly conceived vocationalism and vocationalised a liberal tradition which had too often ignored relevance to the world of work, howsoever that was conceived.

TVEI has been a vehicle for the introduction of a far greater emphasis on the practical and the productive ways of knowing which resonates with John Dewey's criticisms, i.e. the tendency for school teaching to separate theory from practice and thinking from doing.

The school curriculum

Underpinning the legislative changes can be discerned a deeply rooted ideology of what education should be. Raymond Williams (1961, p. 147) succinctly states:

> Schematically one can say that a child must be taught: first, the accepted behaviour and values of his society; second, the general knowledge and attributes appropriate to the educated man; and third, a particular skill by which he will earn his living and contribute to the welfare of his society.

The spirit of that ideology is seen in Section 1 of the Education Reform Act 1988; it places a statutory responsibility on the schools to provide a broad and balanced curriculum which promotes the spiritual, moral, cultural, mental and physical development of pupils and prepares them for the opportunities, responsibilities and experiences of adult life.

Unfortunately, the political decision − to choose the ten subjects specified and to legislate what counts as knowledge within these subjects − does not offer the kind of structure that promotes a balance between the theoretical, practical and productive ways of knowing. Instead the emphasis on content to be learnt has been determined by what will be assessed through national subject tests at regular intervals in the pupils' school lives. However, identifying links and building connections between the subjects in a way that enables the learner to integrate new knowledge into his/her already existing belief system may help to redress the balance.

The cross-curricular elements have been articulated as being an important factor in providing this broad and balanced curriculum. They are perceived as a 'bridging device' in a number of different ways. One way is to define cross-curricular as a dimension, i.e. an approach to learning that permeates the whole curriculum, and the NCC document

(1990a) cites equal opportunities as a key dimension. The spirit and ethos of the school should promote all children to realize their potential, whatever their sex, social, cultural or linguistic background. Skills are another aspect of what the NCC document (1990a) perceives as cross-curricular, and by this is meant generic skills, relevant to all the subjects, e.g. communication skills (oracy, literacy), numeracy, problem-solving, study skills, personal and social skills, and information technology (IT).

Five themes are identified by the NCC document (1990a) as essential and substantive cross-curricular elements: health education; environment; citizenship; economic and industrial understanding; and careers education and guidance. The notion of a theme is a bundle of concepts that cohere, utilizing subject knowledge taught with personal knowledge and experience in order to grapple with real-life issues. The concept of cross-curricular themes within the National Curriculum framework opens up possibilities and opportunities for young people to become actively engaged in interdisciplinary inquiry. When the learner is able to apply knowledge to practical situations, s/he experiences the intrinsic worth of knowing. The next chapter considers these cross-curricular elements in more detail.

Chapter 2

THE CROSS-CURRICULAR
ELEMENTS

Chapter 1 described the structure of the National Curriculum,
explaining that ten subjects now make up the statutory
requirement. What these ten subjects contain in terms of
knowledge, understanding and skills to be taught was determined by individual working parties set up by the Secretary
of State for Education. This method of deciding what was to
be taught was a departure from curriculum tradition in English and Welsh education. Previously any curriculum change
and development had taken place principally by innovative
teachers working in schools or for the local education authorities, or by organizations in which practising teachers played
a key role. Particularly over the last three decades, the rapid
expansion of the comprehensive school initiated curriculum
development programmes. Alternative forms and structures
of learning were introduced – alongside the more traditional
academic subjects – to reflect important changes in the fabric
of our society.

In the absence of a National Curriculum, the 1960s and
1970s was a time when innovations flourished in both primary
and secondary schools, wherever expertise, resources and
enthusiasm were available. Organizations – such as the
Schools Council, departments of education in universities and
colleges of higher education, teacher associations, LEAs,
interest groups and pressure groups – facilitated and supported school curriculum developments through research, by
giving teachers opportunities to develop new ideas, by pub-
lishing materials and by running in-service courses and conferences to disseminate ideas and share experiences. New
ideas of what should be taught included new ideas of how it
should be taught. In essence, this involved a different relation-

ship between teacher and pupil, which emphasized making knowledge relevant to the pupils' lives and involving them in practical and productive tasks. Rural studies, environmental studies, social studies, humanities, drama, business studies, active tutorial work, careers, health education, political studies, peace studies, industrial experience, European studies, economics and computer science are examples of the kinds of experiences pupils were offered in many secondary schools. These existed alongside the traditional school subjects: English, mathematics, science, history, geography, art, music, physical education, home economics, technical subjects, foreign languages and religious education. Within primary schools, learning organized around topics took hold. These topics acted as themes to link the different subject areas in an inter-disciplinary way, taking up about a third to half a term's work – with titles such as 'darkness and light,' 'invasions', 'space', 'toys', 'victorians', 'conservation', 'food,' 'survival,' 'water', 'communication', 'war and peace', and 'materials' – and existed alongside reading, writing and number work.

In contrast to this move towards interdisciplinary teaching structures, the National Curriculum emphasizes subject knowledge. Also, what was considered suitable for teaching at different ages was decided by subject committees that included practising teachers only as a minority group. Each subject committee reported to the Secretary of State independently, with final decisions about the subject content and structures being taken by him after a period of consultation. There was no attempt, during the development stage, to look across the individual subjects and ascertain the total picture of what would be the experience of the individual pupil. When the core and foundation subject documents were made available it became clear that many areas of learning that had taken hold in many schools were not part of the statutory requirements. It became apparent that, by deciding on ten statutory subjects, many knowledge areas and educational experiences thriving in schools were in danger of being crowded out of the curriculum.

The NCC, a government-appointed body, was given the task of addressing this issue. Its curriculum guidance booklet (NCC 1990a), sent free to all schools, emphasized that the core and foundation subjects were not the whole curriculum and that the curriculum should also include what they termed cross-curricular elements. Given that all maintained schools are now party to the National Curriculum requirements, this chapter makes use of the advice documents – a series of documents published by the NCC – as a useful framework with which to explore cross-curricular work going on in schools.

Cross-curricular elements

The cross-curricular elements play a particular role in the whole school curriculum. Primarily, they are concerned with the processes that contribute to the personal development and social awareness of young people i.e. they are concerned not only with mental development – children knowing about aspects of the world about them – but also emotional and attitudinal development – understanding the effect of that knowledge on what is happening in everyday life. Thus, each child is a proactive participant in the learning process; they are encouraged to think about themselves in relation to the world about them, to have ideas about things and to share them, to develop a self-image whilst at the same time empathizing and being aware of the thoughts and feelings of others, and to see themselves as part of a community and to understand what that community values.

The learner is facilitated by the teacher through a variety of techniques; each child moves along different paths of thinking and explorations of ideas that they construct for themselves in a non-threatening learning environment. The cross-curricular elements have been usefully sub-divided by the NCC (1990a) into dimensions, skills and themes. The dimensions create the climate in the school for learning and the cross-curricular skills provide the tools for each learner to create express and articulate knowledge, understanding and experiences. The cross-curricular themes connect the trans-

21

mission of each subject's orthodoxy of ideas and processes with human values, beliefs and qualities that govern the way knowledge is applied in everyday life. Through discussing these three elements in more detail, a context is provided for understanding the case studies of cross-curricular teaching and learning practices described in the following two chapters.

Cross-curricular dimensions

Cross-curricular dimensions create the climate in a school for learning, and equal opportunities underpins this cross-curricular element.

> Equal opportunities is about helping all children to fulfil their potential. Teachers are rightly concerned when their pupils under-achieve and are aware that educational outcomes may be influenced by factors outside the school's control such as a pupil's sex or social, cultural or linguistic background (NCC 1990a, p. 2).

The school, as a social institution, is the structure in which equal opportunities has to operate. The school is organized by professional people, trained to use their knowledge, skills, understanding, values and attitudes to develop and draw out the best in the young people sent to them. Those teachers, with the support staff and pupils, become a community of individuals that must work together within a bounded environment, and that environment then takes on an identity of its own. Attitudes towards others – whatever their sex, class, ethnic origin or ability – determine the way individuals then interact with one another, and this results in the sensing of the climate of a school, and the feelings about what is acceptable practice in that school. After visiting a school people may say things like 'that school is so friendly'; 'this school seems to care about its pupils', 'that school has a sense of excitement about it' and so on. The school seems to take on a persona; radiates an ethos which results from the way people within the school act towards each other.

A school is concerned with learning, and with knowledge, so it might be compared to a library with the teacher being like a textbook from which the pupil learns. However, as a

22

dynamic living entity composed of many different interacting people, all offering their unique contribution to any given situation, the school is more like a vast communications network than an inert silent library. All sorts of messages travel to and fro in this network stimulating responses and activities, and the kind of messages sent out by the controllers of the system can affect the receivers' actions in a positive way. The cross-curricular dimension of equal opportunities encourages non-discriminatory messages being received by students, which enhances the relationships between students and those between students and teachers. This can then result in better quality learning experiences for all children being on offer in the school structure.

The process of establishing an equal opportunities policy in the school also alerts teachers to the need to be conscious of meeting the different needs of children. The equal opportunities policy supports the implementation of the National Curriculum, giving each child a fair chance – by offering them the full range of the curriculum but at an appropriate level so that they can achieve – as well as providing a variety of ways of learning that encourages them to give of their best.

One strategy is to introduce differentiation in the classroom. Weston (1992) offers a helpful and constructive definition: differentiation is the process of identifying with each learner, the most effective strategies for achieving agreed targets. So, all learners have their own targets and these have been made clear to them. The implication here is that some of the responsibility for learning rests on the child, to manage his/her own learning. In such a classroom structure, there is a different relationship between the teacher and the class; it is more collaborative with children working more independently, through agreed tasks, either on their own or with others. The learning becomes more than reading, listening and writing: the learners solve problems together and support each other in developing ideas by talking together; they use röle play to empathize with the way other people see things and engage in simulations that model real-life situations; they construct

23

useful products and interact with the community through work placements and community projects.

Boys and girls are encouraged to feel that they need not adhere to stereotypical roles if they prefer not to, without fear of being ridiculed. No longer is it acceptable for them to be told by teachers or peers, for example, 'Girls do not become engineers' or 'That is a soppy thing for a boy to do'. In a climate of equal opportunities, each individual can develop intellectually, emotionally and aesthetically in a way that celebrates his or her own personal talents and qualities, regardless of gender.

Britain is now considered to be a pluralistic society, with citizens from a variety of cultural and religious backgrounds, and the equal opportunities dimension pays heed to this situation. The school culture can be enriched by tapping the resources of cultural diversity in the surrounding community in a positive and instructive way. The school provides a unique and supportive environment in which pupils can develop the qualities of tolerance and sensitivity, by learning from one another in an environment that promotes equity and justice.

Respect for all should permeate the equal opportunities policy as put into practice in the school. This, along with professionally structured teaching programmes initiated by the teachers that include children actively engaging in learning, should create a climate in the school that promotes positive attitudes to gender equality, cultural diversity and special needs of all kinds.

Cross-curricular skills

The following skills are transferable, being chiefly independent of content and thus able to be developed in different contexts across the whole curriculum:

- communication,
- numeracy,
- study,
- problem-solving,

- personal and social, and
- information technology (IT).

The NCC's (1990a, p. 3) document, *The Whole Curriculum*, states that 'much of the future is uncertain; what is beyond dispute is that in the next century these skills, together with flexibility and adaptability, will be at a premium'. For quality living, in a modern complex society, these highlighted core skills are somewhat fundamental. A useful way to consider them is to reframe them as active verbs instead of abstract nouns. To be skilled implies the need for practice to improve one's ability to do things well, so we could say that for pupils to improve their ability they need regular practical guided training in communicating, calculating, studying, problem-solving, working with other people as part of a team and using a computer. As they become more skilled, less guided instruction should be necessary, thus increasing the facility for pupils to direct and support their own learning. They would know how to organize their work, access information, calculate correctly, work in harmony with others and speak and write appropriately in different situations.

It is believed that the practical skills are best learnt when they are utilized in a knowledge context, i.e. when their use has relevance for achieving an outcome of importance to the learner. If we want or children to be skilled at more than passive listening, reading and writing, then the teacher has to incorporate other strategies into his/her teaching repertoire which will make it possible for the pupils to communicate orally and physically and visually, to identify and wrestle with solving problems, to actively engage in team work so as to develop their social skills, and to be given the kind of home-work that encourages them to organize and manage independent learning. Not every teacher would cover all these aspects but if a school has an overall policy on skill acquisition then the pupils will receive a balance of the necessary training in the core skills across their curriculum.

It is easy to assume that children will pick up these skills as part of everyday life in the classroom, and it is fair to say that many do, given that opportunities and resources are available with which to practise. However, generally speaking, expertise is enhanced when all teachers accept the responsibility for direct training and guidance in these core skills. Such an approach is in keeping with the spirit of equal opportunities discussed earlier. The teacher therefore operates on two levels: at one level, s/he is teaching new knowledge, principles, concepts, ideas and so on, in a way that enables the pupils to practise at least some of the core skills; at another level s/he is observing the pupils' working practices, diagnosing each pupil's competence in these skills and then deliberately guiding their development in skills acquisition. The case-study examples of classroom practice that follow this chapter show some of the ways that knowledge and skill acquisition in a climate of equal opportunities can take place.

Cross-curricular themes

The interaction of knowledge acquired by the child and that child developing his/her own understanding, attitude and skills is a central tenet of the cross-curricular themes specifically mentioned by the NCC (1990a): citizenship, environment, economic and industrial understanding, health education and careers education and guidance. These particular themes were not NCC constructions; their foundations lie in the innovative practices mentioned in the introduction that have been going on in schools over a number of years. The Curriculum Guidance documents (NCC 1990a-f) provide a format for expressing and prioritizing particular learning experiences, from the diversity of developments, that on consideration should be incorporated into the school curriculum in order to render it broad, balanced and relevant. The perception is that since these knowledge themes deal with social knowledge, human affairs and everyday issues opportunities exist to make learning for the pupils useful, relevant and worthwhile: useful because they can use the knowledge to make decisions about everyday life; relevant because it concerns the construction of personal meaning and understanding about complex issues;

and worthwhile because it encourages young people to look around them, to understand the responsibilities that human beings have in looking after the planet and to recognize that human actions have consequences.

Each theme has two attributes: one attribute is concerned with propositional knowledge learning *about* the theme; the other is the explicit inclusion of the interrelationship between knowledge and values – learning *through* the theme. Each theme is a bundle of concepts that interrelate, held rationally and logically together to describe and explain aspects of the overarching theme and taking concepts from the subject disciplines that feed into that theme. Learning through a theme, the child finds out new facts, ideas, points of view and principles about how people act in the world, managing the environment, the health of people in society, how work is organized, how social systems work and so on. However, each theme is also concerned with growth of personal qualities, attitudes, values and behaviour. If attention is paid to the child's personal value and belief system within a teaching environment committed to democratic principles such as rationality, fairness, tolerance and respect of others, the child begins to understand that knowledge and values are intrinsically intertwined in the area of social affairs and so begins to relate personal values with those around him/her.

For young people, the working citizens of the future to live a full and healthy existence in a democratic society, they need to begin, whilst still at school, to appreciate what constitutes the structure of our democratic process. They need to understand why there are different points of view on a whole range of social and moral issues, and they need to recognize that, as individuals, they are neither completely free to do as they please nor completely controlled by the society of which they are a part. Within a democracy, being proactive developing and taking control over one's life, is possible when one is equipped with the knowledge, the skills, values and attitudes to participate fully. Together, the themes of citizenship, environmental education health education, economic and industrial understanding, and careers education and guidance make up the major areas of social life and experience to be addressed within any education system committed to democratic principles. A summary of what constitutes each of these themes and indications of the curriculum developments and practices from which they have emerged, now follows.

Citizenship

Education for citizenship has its roots in the school subject of social studies i.e. study of the individual in society to gain an understanding of the social environment within which people develop as citizens. Social studies draws its concepts mainly from the disciplines of sociology, social psychology and politics. Political education, as such, did not break through to become a popular school subject – owing to the apolitical stance taken by schools that did not wish to engage in such value-laden and controversial issues. Whitty (1985) considers this to be because we conceive of ourselves living in a relatively stable society, one that is generally liberal and humanistic, so we prefer to socialize young people implicitly into the status quo. Hargreaves (1982) believes that schools have been given double messages by politicians who, suspicious of party politics in school, have not supported and encouraged developments to democratize school structures and educate young people to become politically literate. However, some of the persuasive ideas disseminated by advocates for political education have influenced many teachers and can be found in school programmes of general studies, social studies, personal and social education (PSE) and lifeskills courses.

The argument for providing political education is that if we believe our democracy depends on well-informed and responsible adults aware of how the democratic system operates – how decisions are made, the procedures of lawmaking and law enforcement, the structure of local and national government and the balance of duties, rights and responsibilities within the system – then these things cannot be left to chance, but must be explicitly taught to young people.

In 1974, the Nuffield Foundation funded a political education project, which articulated four main features of political education: a very broad conception of politics to include group behaviour at school and in everyday life; political issues as the focus of teaching to consider what should be done; why, how, and when people disagree; and an emphasis on developing both political concepts and acquiring practical knowledge and politically relevant skills. Also, in 1985, the Law Society and the School Curriculum Development Committee established a 'Law in Education' project; they state that:

> the law touches on many issues of a controversial and political nature where differing views are sincerely held by reasonable members of society. It is important therefore, that young people be encouraged to recognise this fact and to think through their own ideas on appropriate matters and to be able to hold them and defend them with reasoned argument.

The structure of the NCC citizenship theme reflects these debates on political education and utilizes some of the ideas developed in these two projects. It seeks to strike a balance between general social and community issues and the process and procedures of political structures. It encourages the notions of active citizenship, stressing the importance of presenting controversial issues in a balanced way and citing the Education (no. 2) Act 1986, which places duties on LEAs, governing bodies and headteachers to forbid partisan political activities in primary schools and the promotion of partisan political views in the teaching of any subject in all schools. It states 'where political issues are brought to the attention of pupils, there is a duty to secure that they are offered a balanced presentation of opposing views (NCC 1990f: 14).

In more recent times, the notion of citizenship has been tackled by a parliamentary commission set up by the then Speaker of the House of Commons, Sir Bernard Weatherill. The aim of the commission was to consider how best to encourage, develop and recognize 'active citizenship' within a wide range of groups in the community, both local and national including school students, adults, those in full employment, as well as volunteers. The commission reported in July 1990 and made a number of recommendations of which learning to be a citizen was a top priority. In summarizing the issues the report states:

> lack of knowledge can be a major obstacle to proper participation in society ... the challenge to our society in the late twentieth century is to create conditions where all who wish can become actively involved, can understand and participate in the making of decisions, can work together for the mutual good.

To this end the first section of the recommendations is entitled 'learning to be a citizen' and recommendation one states (Speaker's Commission 1990, p. xix)

> The Commission recommends that the study and experience of citizenship should be part of every young person's education whether in state or private sector schools, irrespective of the course of study being followed, and from the earliest year of schooling and continuing into the post school years within further and higher education and the youth service.

The Commission took evidence on a number of studies investigating the issue of citizenship, school curriculum and the views of young people. In this way they informed and influenced the NCC before the guidance on citizenship in schools was circulated.

Education for citizenship within the National Curriculum structure is concerned with developing the knowledge, skills and attitudes necessary for exploring, making informed decisions about and exercising responsibilities and rights in a democratic society. Citizenship is perceived as, not some abstraction that is merely talked about, but a state of being, experienced day by day. Approaches to education for citizenship are expressed by understanding it as interweaving knowledge with process through the practical and productive ways of knowing, i.e. the individual draws from real-life situations: the family, the school and the community. Development of concepts, inherent in being a citizen, is acquired through the pupils engaging in practical learning experiences: pupils find out what they need to know in order to complete the activity and then reflect on and discuss the experience after it has taken place. Interactive and proactive activities give them opportunities to engage in observing, organizing, identifying, discussing and debating. The NCC suggest two overall aims:

1. to establish the importance of positive, participative citizenship and provide the motivation to join in (education through citizenship); and
2. to help pupils to acquire and understand essential information on which to base the development of their skills, values and attitudes towards citizenship (education about citizenship).

They suggest eight essential knowledge content components. Three explore broad areas:

- the nature of community;
- roles and relationships in a pluralist society; and
- the duties, responsibilities and rights of being a citizen.

The other five are more context-specific, grounded in the everyday need for citizenship in the present and future lives of pupils:

- the family;
- democracy in action;
- the citizen and the law;
- work, employment and leisure; and
- public services.

These components naturally integrate in a number of ways with some cross-referencing to other themes: the family with health education; and work, employment and leisure with health education, economic and industrial understanding and careers education and guidance. Positive attitudes and values that correspond with democratic principles are addressed through activities that promote a range of personal qualities such as:

31

- independence of thought on social and moral issues;
- enterprise and persistence in approaching tasks and challenges;
- constructive interest in, and a positive approach to, community affairs;
- a sense of fair play, including respect for the processes of law and the rights of others;
- respect for different ways of life, beliefs, opinions and ideas;
- respect for rational argument and non-violent ways of resolving conflict;
- an active concern for human rights;
- appreciation of democratic decision-making;
- an ability to examine evidence and opinions to form conclusions;
- willingness to discuss and consider solutions to personal, social and moral dilemmas;
- appreciation that distinguishing between right and wrong is not always straightforward; and
- appreciation that personal experience may influence changes in individual's values, beliefs and moral codes.

Environmental education

The development of science and technology has enabled research into the ecological and environmental condition of our world; such research projects mushroomed in the second half of this century within countries of the developed world. Environmental matters are of international concern, and an international perspective was initiated and is supported by the United Nations through UNESCO. The media disseminate the findings of researchers, and this has increased awareness, as citizens of many countries become more and more conscious of the effect that humanity, through its political, economic and social structures as well as its technological and industrial systems is having on the ecological balance and the natural resources of the planet. By the late 1960s and early 1970s, stimulated by increased global awareness of the issues, environmental educational programmes were being advocated at all levels of education: schools, colleges and universities.

There was a sense of environmental crisis, well exemplified by the letter to Europeans from the Secretary General of the Council of Europe that launched European Conservation year in 1970.

> Pollution is here for all of us to see, smell and taste. Water is often unfit to drink. Smoke and fumes attack our lungs. Our nervous systems are under severe strain from noise. Waste products, some partially indestructible, build up faster and faster. In many places soil is eroded away. Landscapes are spoiled and the variety of wildlife gets less every day. All this is happening throughout the world, but more than anywhere in our own densely populated continent. If it goes on much longer, Europe will be uninhabitable. This is not scaremongering. We are facing hard facts – facts discussed by all our nations at a conference organised in Strasbourg last February.

Environmental awareness in England followed that of the international community and it was at this time that environmental studies began to emerge as a subject in the secondary curriculum. Environmental studies courses were developed and taught mainly by geography and biology teachers, alongside the traditional subject studies, although they never fully replaced them.

The environmental studies courses drew on many of the concepts of humanistic geography. A central concept was a 'sense of place': 'To be human is to live in a world filled with significant places' (Relph, 1982). Place is defined as involving qualities of authenticity, character, distinctiveness, personal significance and meaning. Relph contrasts place with placelessness: abstract places that have no personal meaning or significance either because they have not been directly experienced or because they are monotonously uniform or planned without feeling. This concept of place highlights the 'affective bond' between people and places and raises the importance of the effect that our environment has on our feelings, which in turn impoverishes or enriches the quality of our lives. It is this organizing principle about environment that features so prominently in the NCC (1990e) articulation of education for the environment. The stated aims are to:

33

- provide opportunities to acquire the knowledge, values, attitudes, commitment and skills needed to protect and improve the environment;
- encourage pupils to examine and interpret the environment from a variety of perspectives – physical, geographical, biological, sociological, economic, political, technological, historical, aesthetic, ethical and spiritual; and
- arouse pupils' awareness and curiosity about the environment and encourage active participation in resolving environmental problems.

Through these aims it can be seen that environment has strong links with citizenship because it introduces children to the political processes and encourages them to see themselves as taking an active responsible part in generating a better social environment. A sense of responsibility, about place and about how the actions of individuals and communities can destroy or enhance the life forms that exist in these places, closely interrelates with principles of responsible citizenship.

The NCC suggests that knowledge about environment – as a framework to inform problem-solving and decision-making concerning environmental issues – should consist of:

- natural process that take place in the environment (relating to such topics as climate, soils and water);
- the impact of human activities on the environment (such as buildings, industrialization and waste);
- different environments, both past and present, and how they change;
- environmental issues (such as the greenhouse effect, acid rain, pollution) and conflicts;
- local, national and international legislative controls to protect and manage the environment;
- the environmental interdependence of individuals, groups, communities and nations (such as power station emissions in one country affecting others);

- the importance of planning and aesthetic considerations; and
- the importance of effective action to protect and manage the environment.

Education through environment means engaging in environmental projects at a practical level i.e. actually being involved in projects which affect their immediate environment. Through experience, attitudes and values are shaped hopefully, to:

- appreciate and care for the environment;
- have independence of thought on environmental issues;
- have a respect for the beliefs and opinions of others;
- have a respect for evidence and reasoned argument; and
- be tolerant and open-minded.

Health education

Although health education has been argued as an important and desirable part of the school curriculum it has never really found a place within the curriculum in its own right. The implementation of health-related issues has been part of general science, biology, home economics, physical education and social studies.

What health education should include has been guided by society's concept of health. Present-day society perceives health as both a scientific concept and a valued personal attribute. For a long time, health has been defined as the absence of disease (Sutherland, 1980). This focus on health, labelled the medical model, has been significantly broadened in recent years to encompass the inter-relationship between body and mind, thereby recognizing the centrality of personal attitude and behaviour as well as cultural and environmental influences. The World Health Organization defines health as 'a state of complete physical, mental and social well-being and not merely the absence of infirmity' (WHO, 1978).

Health education is therefore seen today as health promotion, which Horner (1980) defines as the sum total of all influences that collectively determine knowledge, belief and behaviour related to the promotion, maintenance and restoration of health in individuals and communities. This health promotion view has its critics who see it as manipulative and doctrinaire. Certain educationalists claim that, since knowledge is not culture-free, promoting a particular perspective takes away freedom of choice. Baelz (1980) claims that the educator encourages pupils to develop the capacity to think for themselves, while the indoctrinator wishes to make it impossible for pupils ever to question the doctrine that has been taught.

The focus of health education from an educative perspective is the provision of knowledge, the exploration of values and the development of skills so that the individual can make voluntary and informed decisions about how to be healthy, keep healthy and maintain a sense of personal well-being.

Health as espoused by the NCC document reflects the debate about health education and health promotion, attempting to strike a balance between the two. The document takes a lead from the HMI booklet, *Curriculum Matters: Health Education from 5–16.*

- Education for health begins in the home where patterns of behaviour and attitudes influence health for good or ill throughout life and will be established before the child is five. The tasks for schools are to support and promote attitudes, practices and understanding conducive to good health. Insofar as they are able to counteract influences which are not conducive to good health, they should do so with sensitive regard to the relationship which exists between children and their families.

The NCC health education package involves, firstly, education about health: to provide information on what is good and what is harmful, for which eight content areas are recommended:

- psychological aspects of health education;
- family life;

- safety;
- health-related exercise;
- personal hygiene;
- environmental aspects;
- food and nutrition;
- sex education; and
- substance use and misuse.

Secondly, the package involves education through health: to promote quality of life and the physical, social and mental well being of the individual.

In keeping with the philosophy of health education pre-National Curriculum, the document (1990c, p. 7) supports the view that

> if a health education programme is to help pupils to make informed choices, establish a healthy lifestyle and build up a system of values, the teaching methods used are as important as the content of lessons. The participation of pupils is essential in order to encourage pupils to learn from others and to help them use appropriate language in ways that are understood by others.

Economic and Industrial Understanding

Economic and Industrial Understanding (EIU) is a phrase created by the NCC; it has its foundation in the vocational educationalist movement, which called for closer links between the educational system and the economy, to make schools serve the needs of industry more effectively. A key event in the modern development of vocationalism within education was the 1976 speech by the then Labour Prime Minister, James Callaghan, at Ruskin College in which he challenged the educational establishment to be more explicit in preparing and socializing young people for an industrial and technological society:

> the goals of education are clear enough – they are to equip children to the best of their ability for a lively, constructive place in society and also to fit them to do a job of work.

Richard Pring, who has researched and written extensively

37

on the new vocationalism, believes there are four reasons behind Mr. Callaghan's emphasis (Pring 1987, p. 133–4):

> ... firstly, new recruits from the schools sometimes do not have the basic tools to do the job that is required; secondly, there is an anti-industrial spirit especially amongst the most able; thirdly, students were ill-equipped technologically in a society dominated by new technologies; and fourthly, students were not developing those qualities that equip them for making a living.

Discussions about increasing vocational relevance in schools became part of the general educational debate that followed the Ruskin speech and initiatives were set up to build closer liaisons between the world of work and schools. One of these was the well-resourced Technical and Vocational Educational Initiative (TVEI) set up in 1982 and managed by the Manpower Services Commission with funding from the Department of Employment. The objective of TVEI was to provide resources to generate curriculum development work in schools that would make school-industry liaison a practical reality. This project was targeted at the 14–18 age range and work-related curriculum activities were introduced, with pupils also going out on work experience. TVEI focused on greater use of computers and emphasised the development of personal qualities such as initiative, enterprise and responsibility and competence in the skills that industry valued, like numeracy, communications and information technology. A focus on equal opportunities and helping pupils assess their own capabilities in relation to future job and career prospects were also part of the TVEI educational experience.

TVEI and other vocational initiatives have generated heated debate among educationalists, many of whom feel it is important for young people to receive a general education before being primed and trained for industrial, commercial or service occupations. There are arguments about how the term 'vocationalism' ought to be defined and questions about the aims of education in a changing society. Pring (1987, p. 147) puts it like this:

> Preparing future generations for life, which Mr. Callaghan pointed

to as an aim of education, included preparation for the world of work – and to what extent it should be vocational. But this can be interpreted generously – where social awareness includes the capacity for political argument and criticism, where communication skills do not ignore the richness of literature and of experience as a basis of something to communicate about, where teaching respects activity and practically based learning that we know pupils respond to. Or it can be narrowly interpreted where persons are subject trained, where communication is limited to the safe and non-controversial, and where there is an over-emphasis on skills that derive from others' often mistaken view of what the economy needs.

The planning of the curriculum guidance document by the NCC, Jamieson (1991, p. 60) tells us,

> brought together a diverse group of interest groups which included: representatives of the school-industry movement; representatives from various economic awareness/understanding projects (with diverse views about economics and pedagogy; and representatives from the field of business studies.

The make-up of the document reflects these interest groups, bringing together the school-industry work that had been going on with other economic concerns, thereby drawing from the key concepts of economics for the knowledge base of the theme, e.g. concepts such as scarcity, costs, marginality, efficiency and wealth.

The NCC document (1990b, p. 1) puts the EIU aims thus:

> Throughout their lives pupils will face economic decisions. They will face choices about how they contribute to the economy through their work. They will decide how to organise finances and which goods or services to spend money on. They will form views on public issues, such as the environmental effects of economic development or the economic arguments involved in elections.
>
> Education for economic and industrial understanding aims to help pupils to make these decisions. It explores economic aspects of their present lives. It prepares them for future economic roles: as producers, consumers and citizens in a democracy.

Knowledge and understanding about EIU includes:

- key economic concepts such as production, distribution and supply and demand;
- how business enterprise creates wealth for individuals and the community;
- the organization of industry and industrial relations;
- what it means to be a consumer, how consumer decisions are made and the implications of these decisions;
- the relationship between economy and society in different economic systems;
- technological developments and their impact on lifestyles and workplaces; and
- the role of government and international organizations (for example, the European Union) in regulating and providing public services.

Education through EIU should foster analytical, personal and social skills such as:

- the ability to collect, analyse and interpret economic and industrial data;
- thinking carefully about different ways to solving economic problems and making economic decisions;
- distinguishing between fact and value in economic situations;
- communicating economic ideas accurately and clearly; and
- developing skills related to working life, e.g. leading, being enterprising and working sensitively with others.

The document emphasizes the need to develop positive attitudes and values towards economic and industrial affairs. This is to be achieved by active involvement, i.e. through direct experience of industry and the world of work and by engaging in enterprise schemes. This will give young people a sense of responsibility for, and an awareness of, the consequences of their own economic actions and an ability to reflect critically on their own economic views and values and to respect different economic points of view.

Careers education and guidance

Careers education and guidance (CEG), despite having no direct link with a subject discipline from which to draw its knowledge concepts as the other four themes do, is inextricably linked with personal development and social awareness. It is seen as relevant and useful, as well as non-controversial, and ties in with all four cross-curricular themes, particularly with the aspect of EIU concerned with the world of work. Thinking about future prospects is an integral part of vocational education and therefore it is an important part of the TVEI experiences in secondary schools. Prior to the implementation of technical and vocational education in schools, careers was a bit of a Cinderella subject, a bolt-on at the end of a pupil's time in school. In 1971, the Schools Council Careers Education and Guidance project was established. A philosophy about careers education emanated from the project that broadened the scope of careers education, viewing it as more than just about jobs, as a process to help young people recognize what they are capable of and to give them the confidence to take some control over their own lives.

This view of careers education as a process was reiterated by the Department of Education and Science in a 1983 discussion document on careers education. They stated that 'careers education and guidance is not a subject, but a process on which a school needs to have a policy'. They made four points about the way careers education should help pupils:

1. to make them aware of opportunities in education, training and work;
2. to understand themselves in relation to these opportunities;
3. to come to informed and reasoned decisions; and
4. to make the transition between school and work.

A number of other publications followed, including *Working together for a Better Future* (DES/DoE; 1987), *Curriculum Matters 10* (DES 1988), and *Towards a Skills Revolution* (CBI:

41

1989), which encouraged interest in careers guidance in the widest sense. The NCC document *Curriculum Guidance 6* (NCC 1990d) encapsulates the broader perspective on CEG, encouraging close links between teachers and careers officers.

NCC aims for CEG are to help pupils to:

- know themselves better;
- be aware of education, training and careers opportunities;
- make choices about their own continuing education and training, and about career paths; and
- manage transitions to new roles and situations.

The document enumerates what are called strands of development:

- *self* – self-knowledge in relation to potential and limitations;
- *roles* – with particular reference to expectations from family and peers and community;
- *work* – involving an understanding of paid and unpaid work at home and in the community; and
- *transition* – adjusting to, and coping with, change which involves moving into new roles and situations.

The NCC believe that the CEG programme in schools should foster the following attitudes and values:

- a motivation to engage in learning as a life-time process;
- a positive approach to investment in personal growth and development from within;
- personal responsibility in role choice and adoption;
- independence of thought through the challenging of stereotyping, a rational understanding of the need to balance personal aspiration against the availability of opportunities and the exercising of choice within a framework of skills, aptitudes and inclinations against pressure from external sources;

- an appreciation of the changing nature of attitudes towards work and of work itself; and
- concern for human rights in relation to personal growth and development, the maximizing of individual potential and the use of human resources.

Concluding comment

Understanding society is not explicitly stated as part of the subject curriculum but is the central tenet of the cross-curricular themes. Within the whole curriculum their rôle is clear: to socialize young people into a complex industrial and technological world. It would be difficult not to argue that knowledge about the workings of Parliament and local government, of the law, of the organization of industry, of public administration and the effects that humanity has on the natural world is at least as relevant as the content within the subject knowledge curriculum. The education system has a responsibility to help young people come to a meaningful understanding of societal issues, to encourage them to be active citizens, decision-makers and independent thinkers, conscious of the effect of the values and attitudes they hold on others and on the quality of their lives. Within the structured situation of school, teachers as educators constantly try to draw out the best in their pupils. The following case studies of cross-curricular practices in primary and secondary schools show some of the ways teachers work towards this ideal.

Chapter 3

CROSS-CURRICULAR ELEMENTS; PRIMARY PRACTICE

Although primary schools have always been concerned with the basic skills of reading, writing and numeracy, they have also been concerned with the well-being of the children. Many primary teachers have developed teaching methods that draw out the interests of the child and use these interests as a motivating factor to extend the children's knowledge base, whilst at the same time helping them to develop as people. The integrated project work that has served as an organizing structure for teaching and learning within primary schools since the 1960s is alive and well within the National Curriculum although there is now a political force pushing these schools towards greater concentration on subject teaching. However, for some schools, the National Curriculum has given this mode of curriculum organization a new lease of life; many see the framework of the National Curriculum attainment targets (ATs) and programmes of study (PoS) as a device that introduces more rigour and definable targets into their teaching programmes without preventing them from continuing to work in a thematic way.

There may be as many different approaches to learning as there are schools. While a number of different primary schools were visited in preparing this chapter, they all share a discernible attitude towards children and education. The culture and ethos of these primary schools is about teachers defining learning as more than an understanding of content or of technological processes; they consider the curriculum as a communications network and are concerned about the messages transmitted on the 'airwaves' of the learning environment.

This attitude has the effect that teachers emphasize the importance of the pupils themselves posing and asking questions and considering and reflecting on key questions about issues that arise from the social context in which they live. Before going into particular examples of practice, it is worth describing two primary school approaches that exemplify this cultural trait. Ide and Cowick.

Ide

The first example is a village first school. It is warm, friendly, colourful and inviting, with three classrooms opening into one another and a large part of the space in each classroom divided into resource areas clearly marked: Reading, Mathematics, Science, Technology. The hall is set out with musical instruments on tables, play equipment and a puppet theatre. The walls are covered with brightly coloured displays of pupils work and stimulus resource material.

The structure of the school day reflects the centrality of the principles of personal development, social awareness and equal opportunities that permeate every aspect of this first school's curriculum.

The guiding principle is based on a humanistic educational approach introduced into Britain from America and called High/Scope. It is believed that children as young as 4 years old are capable of making decisions and solving problems about activities that are of interest to them. Teachers use these personal interests as a springboard to motivate pupils and to challenge them, teaching them both social and academic concepts.

The teacher's approach to learning, the climate s/he engenders in the classroom and the way s/he relates to the pupils is an active realization of respect for pupil's ideas, actions and modes of thinking. Within the school day, there is a balance between teacher-initiated (circle time – small group work time – outside time) and pupil-initiated activities (planning time – workshop time – recall time). The children spend time planning what they are going to do, writing their plans in a

45

planning book. They are then given time to follow through their plans and are expected to review what they have done with the teacher and their peers. The children are never talked at, but interact with the teacher and each other, learning through experience, learning how to articulate, communicate and conceptualize their experiences.

In order to meet the pre-specified objectives within the key stages of the National Curriculum, the teachers have to be particularly skilled at assessing and appraising children's development, although a good percentage of the school day is given over to the children who engage in learning activities initiated by themselves. The daily routine of planning, doing and reviewing intensifies children's involvement and ownership of the curriculum; it also allows the teacher to stand back, to observe, to be a partner not a leader, and to use dialogue and formative questioning, thus encouraging children to be more resourceful, less adult-dependent and much more communicative in purposeful terms. The teachers believe that this methodology brings out individual differences and underlines the different developmental stages in the class group. This in turn means that the teacher builds his/her teaching on recognition of these differences, thus making it possible to value (socially) and develop (intellectually) each and every child.

Cowick

The following extract from the words of the headteacher (interviewed in 1992) describes a school that has developed an outdoor classroom which provides an external environment to match the richness of the internal one. Within three years of acquiring a piece of waste ground bordering the school, there now exists an outdoor place for extension of classroom work and for imaginative, energetic and purposeful play.

Our philosophy at Cowick is that once inside the school gates our families have entered a place which at every turn expresses our commitment to quality learning. We hope it is obvious that we offer exciting opportunities for active learning in an environment which is a world in miniature.

The only environment for which a first school can properly ask its children to take full responsibility is that of school. The richer that environment, the greater the opportunity exists for learning. We work in partnership with families and the local community, people drawn in who can share children's enthusiasms and stimulate the question asking and can help to seek out the answers from a variety of sources, so that learning can be extended and built upon.

Living growing things are celebrated in our outdoor classroom. We have a wide variety of trees, shrubs, flowers and grasses. Caring for them and observing them throughout the year teaches so much about the cycle of the seasons. Conservation is a word in every child's vocabulary as we cherish each flower and grass that we nurture. There is a kitchen garden in our grounds to help us know the wonder of seeds and the roots, shoots, stems and leaves we eat. Organic growing is part of our everyday life as children bring waste vegetable matter from their homes each day to go on the compost heap.

We care for hens, rabbits and guinea pigs, knowing the responsibility they bring to our lives, cleaning, grooming and generally caring for them. We know the economics of saying 'I want a pet', for we cost food, housing and veterinary bills. And our young scientists know a great deal about that part of the National Curriculum that comes under 'the variety and process of life'. We have a pond and the sort of area that is grandly named a three-canopied habitat (tree shelter, shrub shelter, herbage) so that birds and mini beasts will have a home with us.

As well as the conservation and kitchen gardens we have an area we like to call 'the hide and seek garden'. It is a place for young explorers to plan routeways. Spatial awareness grows as they go round and over the hills and through the tunnels. In the hide and seek garden the geographer meets the historian as the children climb the different gradients and plan the best place to build a castle. Children can run and climb, slide and balance, hide, chase and be caught in the ground. Opportunities for physical challenge abound or they can sit on stiles and logs on a summer's day and dream awhile.

The core and foundation subjects of the National Curriculum are already broad. However, there seems to be no need to fear overload when cross-curricular themes, like environmental education and citizenship, are added if these additions can prove to be a highly suitable vehicle to deliver parts of other programmes of study. That this particular curriculum delivery approach, our outdoor classroom, is also real, meaningful, exciting and relevant to the children's lives is a delightful bonus.

The general philosophy that permeates the culture of these two schools and the schools from which the forthcoming examples are taken have a number of common characteristics.

1. inter-active communication skills are promoted.
2. Creativity is encouraged, expressed through the acceptance of children's ideas and giving them opportunities to express themselves in different ways and through different media.
3. Lots of opportunities are built in to work as part of a team – sharing, caring, looking beyond self-interest – to develop a sense of healthy interdependence with others.
4. Building on the inquisitiveness, interest and natural energy of the children is a paramount consideration.

Five examples of primary practice are now given that concentrate on one or two of the cross-curricular themes, skills and dimensions. They give a flavour of the way that cross-curricular elements act as a connecting device between different forms of knowledge as well as between knowledge and personal development and social awareness. These five cases are typical of an active and experiential learning model designed to foster connections between cognitive and affective knowing. In simple terms the model of learning looks like this:

problem/question

interactive communication—practical activities

significant event

First, questions are raised, or problems articulated, that grow out of the learning that has been going on in the classroom.

Second, the teacher involves the class in the issue of answering the question or solving the problem. S/he encourages lots of talk and the sharing of ideas; children ask questions and so generate purposeful interactions between the teacher and the pupils and between the pupils.

Third, at some point in the on-going interactive communication of ideas engagement in active tasks takes place. The teacher provides the resources and during the activities s/he offers facilitative support in concept formation and application of skills. The pupils, while being actively engaged in being both practical and productive, discuss the problem, collaborate with one another, try out ideas, create and develop, discard and modify all of which leads to a greater understanding, linking proposition knowledge with practical experience, or to put it another way, theory with practice. In this sense, interactive communication and practical activities are in constant association with each other.

Fourth, there is a significant event which acts as a culmination of the activities, an end piece to generate a sense of satisfaction and completion of a module or a cycle of learning. The end product is a real situation and involves participation with and/or contact with people in the outside community.

The examples that follow are a living expression of that descriptive model. It is true to say that such an approach is not the only way that cross-curricular themes can be 'embedded' in the bloodstream of the school. However, approaching cross-curricular work in this way has proved to be particularly effective in galvanizing, exciting and motivating pupils who, as a result of their involvement, feel a strong sense of self-esteem. It is education that fosters positive values, showing how the school communication network goes beyond the classroom and stretches the children to express their knowledge, understanding and human capabilities to the community.

Example 1: 'African Games' at Ipplepen Primary School

Résumé

This project shows how a piece of creative work acts in a cross-curricular way, focusing on the theme of citizenship and the cross-curricular dimension of equal opportunities: race.

Africa, the theme for a term's work for Year 6 (top juniors in the primary school), took up about 50 per cent of the timetable and incorporated National Curriculum programmes of subject study. The children not only learnt about Africa, e.g. the geography of the continent, the history of its development and the climatic conditions that affected food production, but also were encouraged to respond affectively to the material presented, to relate to what they were learning, to talk about their feelings and to think about the difference it made to them to know about these things.

The term's work eventually focused on the country of South Africa, the relationships between the different races that make up the population and the legal structures within which the people lived: apartheid. The significant event that culminated the project was a twenty-minute musical theatre piece called 'African Games'.

Problem/question

The general orientating question, perceived by the teacher as the personal, social and moral dimension of the term's work, was: 'How does it feel to be different?' Over time, as the project evolved, a more specific question framed the creative work with regard to humankind and the equal opportunity issue of racism. Is this black-white relationship fixed in instinct, as in the predator-prey relationship in the jungle, or is humankind capable, through its superior intellect, of effecting change to improve the situation?

Interactive communication

Throughout the project communications between the teacher and pupils remained open and also involved interaction with AOTs (adults other than teachers). The project spilled over from class-time: there was a school happening – a special lunch where the children experienced the fact that three-quarters of the world population does not get enough food. Three out of every four children lining up for school dinner received only a bowl of rice and a drink of water. The lucky quarter, representing the developed nations, had the best school dinner ever produced. All this was designed to make the children experience, as well as think about, issues. The children also participated in a week's residential and out-of-class-time rehearsals for the dramatic event, which included parental contributions. During the term, particular attitudes and values were communicated, fitting within the citizenship theme of roles and relationships in a pluralistic society:

- independence of thought on social and moral issues;
- a sense of fair play;
- active concern for human rights;
- tolerance and open-mindedness;
- recognition of the environmental interdependence of individuals, groups and communities;
- enterprise and persistence in approaching tasks and challenges; and
- willingness to respect the legitimate interests of others.

Practical tasks

Many practical tasks that developed knowledge, understanding and skills took place. The particular skills prioritized were communication, numeracy, problem-solving and personal and social skills, and as for knowledge and understanding, the following task descriptions give some indication of key activities.

- The project began with a week's residential course at Paignton Zoo. This experiential educational visit was structured to go beyond finding out about the animals and observing them objectively. The children considered how the animals behaved in their natural habitat and concepts such as predator/prey, attack/defence, camouflage and so on. The zebra and the lion, in particular, were studied: how they evolved, survived and adapted to the environment.
- A mathematics task was the collection and interpretation of statistics about Africa to compare and contrast African

countries with Great Britain. Also the pupils interpreted graphs of the population of South Africa: whites/coloureds/blacks.

- A science task was experimentation with evaporation and exploration of the food chain.
- A design and technology task was a jungle adventure where the children, after escaping from a plane crash in the jungle, had to design rope bridges to cross ravines and rivers.
- English tasks included creative writing for a purpose and an audience. The children's poetry was included in the final production.

The significant event

'African Games' was an expression in dance and drama of the pupils' understanding of the issue of apartheid; the spoken words were the children's own. It began with a dance showing the predator-prey relationship in the grasslands of Africa, making the point that lions have hunted zebra since creation and they will continue to do so. Such relationships in the animal kingdom are instinctive and incapable of change. Masks were made for the dance, large professional-looking ones. The children learnt the technique from a professional mask-maker. Fifteen zebra moving together in united fear stalked by three hungry lionesses watched over by a regal lion dramatically displayed the law of the jungle. The drama moved from animals to humans and drew a parallel between the animalistic predator-prey relationship and the apartheid system in South Africa. Spoken drama showing the unfairness of the system led into a dance depicting the conflict between blacks and whites.

> Stop what you're saying
> You ignorant brat
> I'm proud of being black
> What's wrong with that?
> Why are white people always the best?
> Just because I've black skin under my vest

> I'm proud of being black
> What's wrong with that?

The whites represented the state police and army. They wore white masks, dominating the blacks, showing an unthinking, uncaring attitude. They acted as if their role was that of the animal predator, superior in strength to their black prey. The blacks reacted, trying to break down barriers, imprisoned by the cage of apartheid from which there was no escape. So the question was asked 'Can change be effected by humankind?' and was then answered by the children in an optimistic way.

Using the theme music from *Chariots of Fire* the whites performed a sports dance based on movements from athletics, rugby and cricket while the blacks looked on. The blacks then performed a dance with the whites looking on. The whites then tore off their masks and danced with the blacks, integrating with them. The masks symbolized domination and their removal symbolized a new unity. Sport was seen as a catalyst for change.

> The blacks and the whites are kept apart
> They should be mind to mind and heart to heart
> Sprinting down the Olympic track
> Black leading white
> White leading black
> The race between black and white ends in a draw
> Heading towards the friendship door
> The swing of the bat
> The heat of the scrum
> The blacks and whites together will come.

This event was performed at the school and then was entered for the Barclays Awards for youth music theatre. It reached the final, which took place in London in November 1992.

The children kept up with the current events in South Africa and understand in their own expressive way the significance of the dismantling of apartheid.

> The world has seen the unfairness
> Of apartheid where black meets white
> The need for integration
> The need for the world to unite
> From the skin colour of someone's face

> To the linking arms of the human race
> But now the world has changed
> Society's rearranged
> We have peeled back this colour of skin
> To realise that we are all the same within.

Example 2: 'Rubbish' at Cowick First School

Résumé

This project shows how links with the neighbourhood community act in a cross-curricular way, focusing on the cross-curricular themes of environment and citizenship.

Rubbish as a thematic umbrella for Year 2 pupils' classroom work acted as a stimulus to generate interest among the pupils in a community re-cycling project, culminating in the setting up of a permanent re-cycling centre in the school grounds. An information board at the re-cycling site states:

> Treat the earth well.
> It was not given to you by your parents.
> It was loaned to you by your children.

Problem/question

The rubbish theme orientated around the investigative question: 'What do we do with rubbish?' and was then extended to: 'What do you need to re-cycle?'

Interactive communication

Challenging and developing the ideas of 7- and 8-year-olds demands skilled teaching; the teacher has to pose the kinds of questions that will stimulate a response to consider things rather than the children just accepting the teacher's word for it. Because the teacher has the control and the power over them, small children are generally eager to please and they can easily come to rely on their teacher to guide their every movement and action. So the teacher has to find the balance between providing a strong framework that gives the children security, (i.e. so that they know the limitations of what is acceptable) while at the same time structuring the classroom

experiences in such a way that the children feel able to introduce their view of things, to follow their lines of enquiry and
to have the confidence to do things their way. This project
exemplifies this kind of balance. The children could not have
had the pleasure of seeing an important idea and vision come
to fruition without the careful managing of all aspects by the
teachers. However, the sensitivity of the teachers towards
their pupils meant that the children had a proper say in the
proceedings and had ownership of the result.

The following attitudes and values were fostered through
this project:

- active concern for human rights;
- discussion and consideration of solutions to personal, social
  and moral dilemmas;
- appreciation that personal experience may influence
  changes in individual values, beliefs and moral codes;
- constructive interest and a positive approach to community
  affairs;
- enterprise and persistence in approaching tasks and challenges;
- recognition of the impact of human activities on the
  environment (relating to waste); and
- appreciation of involvement through effect action to protect
  the environment.

Practical activities

Classroom work on rubbish encompassed learning in many
National Curriculum subject areas.

- Scientific work grew out of collecting litter found on the
  school grounds and analyzing the types found. The litter
  was sorted into different types of materials, e.g. metal,
  plastic, glass and paper. Tests were carried out to discover
  what was biodegradable and what was magnetic. Experi-
  ments were set up to record and investigate rot and decay.
- Mathematical work included number work, (counting items

in dustbins, and the number of dustbins in a street) and for estimating and measuring weight. For example, all the rubbish is saved in a sack; if the rubbish sack weighs 25kg and the rubbish and the sack weigh 75kg, how much does the actual rubbish weigh?

- Geography mapwork involved drawing up the dustbin collector's route, and history tasks involved scrutinizing dustbin 'artefacts of yesterday's rubbish' to distinguish between the old and the new.
- Design and technology tasks consisted of asking the children, for example, can you make a rubbish sorter, a dustbin lorry, or a crusher?
- Creative activities grew out of the question; 'What use can be made of rubbish?' which led to producing junk instruments for music making and junk modelling.
- English work permeated the whole project through continuous questioning and discussion and factual writing, e.g. about visits to shops to find out the kinds of things they threw away. Wall displays were mounted of the scientific, mathematical, historical and geographical work and stories were read relating to rubbish and junk which inspired children to create their own, e.g. if you find a magic lamp in a dustbin, what happens when you rub it clean?

All these activities over a period of time raised the children's awareness of the diversity of rubbish, the range of materials found in dustbins that had a potential for further use. The skills of numeracy, communication and problem-solving were prioritized in these learning tasks, which gave them an understanding about the significance of re-cycling. Information technology and personal and social skills were highlighted when the project moved from the classroom to interacting with the community through an active and meaningful involvement with the re-cycling initiative.

The significant event
Work began on the recycling centre in July 1991. The children decided that they wanted to have a recycling centre at the

school for both public and school use. The school has a small front garden that faces the main road. The Victorian building of the school had been remodelled in 1986 at which time the front door was blocked up. Now, the children neither used nor needed this forecourt, so it seemed a perfect spot. The local waste management officer came to talk to the children and supported their claim. The waste collection bins for clothes, bottles, cans and kitchen waste were then supplied by Exeter City Council. However, a ramp was needed to wheel the bins in and out, so the children wrote to MacDonalds for the money to do this; MacDonalds responded positively and the ramps were subsequently built. The class made posters and leaflets using the school computers. These were printed by William Pollard, a local printing company, and British Telecom donated a noticeboard for the site. So all was in place for the official opening which took place at 10 a.m. on 16 June.

The re-cycling centre at Cowick First School was opened by the Mayor of Exeter. At the opening, three of the children made a speech in front of their peers, their parents and many 'official' dignitaries and visitors.

Alison: We are very grateful that you have all come here on this special day.

Tracey: Why do we want to re-cycle things?

Martin: If we just put things in our dustbins they go to rubbish landfills and one day there won't be any more spaces left.

Tracey: We can't keep digging new materials out of the ground. We might run out of materials.

Alison: Re-cycling things uses less energy. If we use less energy we use less coal. Coal makes smoke and fumes which damages the ozone layer and also pollutes the clouds which rain and pollute rivers and streams.

Tracey: We are persuading people to save re-cycling things by designing posters and leaflets.

Martin: We are also planting flowers around the recycling centre to make it attractive.

Alison: Cowick First School Recycling Centre is helping the
          environment.
All: We want you to help too!!

About a month after the opening the children had a tea party
to thank the local businesses for their help in making the
recycling centre a success. The project received national recognition through receiving the Royal Anniversary Trust's
Schools Award in 1992. Some of the children went to the
Festival Hall to receive it. Alison said, 'We felt very important
sitting in the hall.' She further commented, 'We wanted our
rubbish recycling centre so we can help to save the planet
Earth and because you can save an awful lot of things and
money.'

Example 3: 'The Lovejoy Project' at Irchester Junior School

Résumé

This project shows the close integration of the cross-curricular
themes of citizenship and economic and industrial understanding with the National Curriculum subject of History.
The two teachers of the year 6 classes chose the unit of Victorian England from the programme of study of the National
Curriculum. The teachers wanted to bring history to life and
make it as relevant to the children's own experiences as possible. The 'Lovejoy Project' was conceived to do this. It was an
active practical learning experience that took place towards
the end of the term, drawing on knowledge gained about
Victorian life. The children set up and ran 'An Antiques Roadshow and Auction' for parents, relatives, local business people
and invited members of the LEA.

Problem/question

From a general enquiry about what legacy Victorian England
has left for us today, more specific questions arose around the
concept of value. Why do people value cultural artefacts from
the past? What gives them a value? Who decides?

Interactive communication

This project gave the children the opportunity to interact with people they would not normally expect to meet in their everyday life. Situations were set up that encouraged them to respond, ask questions and experience the enthusiasm adults had for antiques and Victoriana collectable items. Their first such experience was when a young adult, a boy in secondary school, visited them in their classroom. Out of personal interest, he had made a study of their village and brought with him the artefacts that he had collected. His interest and enthusiasm radiated to the children, who were able to handle the artefacts and talk to him about them. A visit to Wilford's, an auctioneer's saleroom, followed with a guided tour from Mr Wilford. They were introduced to a world of work that was totally unfamiliar to them and discovered some of the techniques and skills of valuing articles and selling through an auction. Realizing they would be running an auction themselves they became intrigued and felt motivated to 'have a go'. The classroom work had opened out to involve the children in using the world of work as part of their learning. The children became a working team to put 'the show on the road'.

Attitudes and values nurtured by this experience included:

- an interest in economic affairs;
- respect for evidence in economic contexts;
- enterprise and persistence in approaching tasks and challenges;
- respect for different ways of life, beliefs, opinions and interests;
- appreciation that personal experience may influence changes in an individual's values, beliefs and moral codes; and
- recognition of the valuable contribution people make to the community.

Practical tasks

This practical experience made demands on the children in a number of ways including the learning of new practical skills

- In holding an auction, it was decided the children would make their own artefacts to sell that replicated Victoriana. All the work was productive and creative.
- In terms of the aesthetic, they learnt how to appreciate antiques through a more systematic way of observing, handling and taking note of the details of their construction, design and function.
- They created artefacts – fine art and landscape paintings in miniature style, as were common in Victorian times, which they professionally mounted with skilled help from the art adviser. They also worked in clay and produced small pottery dishes with many different glazes and made Victorian brooches.
- Information technology skills were advanced by using the computer to generate design and lettering for production of the auction catalogue, the invitations, visitors' book and the sale book.
- They applied mathematical skills in sorting the 274 items they had for auction, sequential numbering of the items for the catalogue, calculating the bids and, at the auction itself, establishing the money owed and the correct change. They used estimation when judging from the reply slips how many people would be coming so that they could have sufficient seating and refreshments.
- Personal and social skills were developed through this project and were put to good use on the night of the auction.
- Communication skills were paramount. Written communication skills were put to good use for the correct and succinct description of items in the catalogue, as well as clear and attractive handwriting for the catalogue list. Pupils mingled with adults and guests in professional circumstances, applying their oral skills when welcoming the guests, talking informatively about the proceedings and auctioning their own work.

The significant event

By the time the auction was to take place the whole school had become involved in one way or another. Infected by the activity and excitement of the Year 6 pupils, other classes wanted to make goods for the auction and their teachers helped with the organization. The 'Antiques Auction and Roadshow' took place on 5 December 1991. The evening had two parts. First, there was the roadshow when two invited antiques experts were available to examine and value any items that the guests cared to bring. Children assisted the experts and it was recognized that they had become far more sophisticated about the possible value of objects than they were at the beginning of the project. The second part of the evening was the auction itself. The work was expertly displayed around the auction hall by one teacher who was an art specialist, all items were numbered, corresponding to the 'lots' in the sales catalogue. Many of the children auctioned their own work.

This project was a significant experience for these children – as this written comment from one of them demonstrates. The writer is described by his teacher, and his mother, as a shy boy who holds back and does not communicate easily. This is his account looking back one year later.

Looking back on the 'Lovejoy Project' the things that I enjoyed most were making the different works of art and meeting the new people who came in to show us how to do it. The visit to Wilford's salesroom was interesting. I was not really sure how the auction sales were carried out. The best part of the whole project was the auction which we held at school, at the end of the topic. The excitement built up during the day until Mr. Reynolds arrived to start the evening with valuing people's antiques. It was very interesting listening to the conversations about the antiques. Then the auction began and one by one our works of art were held up. I was nervous when I stood up to auction my painting but as the bidding began I felt more confident. In the end I knocked it down to my sister! I certainly understand how auctions work now.

The Lovejoy project was one of the best topics in the Junior School, with all the school taking part, and I will remember it for a long time, especially for the enjoyment and interest in making and learning about antique objects, the pride of seeing my work displayed and the thrill of the auction. (Greg Arnold, 1992)

Example 4: 'I wish I was there' at Exwick Middle School

Résumé

National Curriculum history became a living exciting experience when the teachers and pupils of Exwick School, in association with a university drama lecturer and his students, trainee teachers, collaborated to develop and broadcast on local radio a play about life in Exwick during World War II. This was a unique way to link cognitive and affective learning through a dramatic medium little used in schools. What makes this project special was the level of professionalism. The play was broadcast on the commercial airwaves with no apology about the fact it involved local schoolchildren.

The school was committed to investigating local history as part of its normal curriculum and was keen to be part of a national history project – 'Dig Where You Stand' – that was encouraging schools, with the offering of a little financial help, to present local historical findings in an artistic form.

The collaboration with the School of Education of the University of Exeter enabled the school's plans to be realized in positive dynamic practice. The play itself was the culmination of a term's work that integrated the National Curriculum subjects of history and English with the cross-curricular themes of citizenship and economic and industrial understanding and cross-curricular skills of communications, problem-solving and personal and social skills.

Problem/question

What is the cultural history of the community? Whose history of World War II is recorded?

Interactive communication

The children had the opportunity to interact with different people on a number of levels. The project had two facets: the learning about the political, social and cultural aspects of life just preceding and during World War II; and the learning through active involvement of how to organize and communicate historical knowledge and understanding. Demands were made on the children to work closely and productively with others, applying understandings and skills they already possessed as well as developing new ones. Through the medium of drama the children came to view and interact with their cultural heritage and the local environment in a new way. The history 'lived again' for these children through the oral histories of surviving members of the community, the school log and the historical artefacts of the period, collected and displayed in the school. To prepare for the drama, they needed a script. In the skilled hands of John Somers, the university drama lecturer, and his students, the pupils improvized, shaped and moulded the historical stories of ex-pupils of the school. The pupils were at the centre of the creative process, party to turning 'raw material' into exciting, structured radio theatre. As John Somers says, 'drama is a powerful cross-curricular activity that benefits the children in all sorts of ways, one of which is enabling pupils to acquire many of the skills required by the National Curriculum'.

The values and attitudes central to the theme of citizenship had many opportunities to find expression in this project:

- an enterprising and persistent approach to tasks and challenges;
- respect for different ways of life, beliefs, opinions and ideas;
- a constructive interest in community affairs; and
- examination of evidence and opinions to form conclusions.

Also, by being involved in a production that was technically operated by professionals, the children experienced what it would be like to work in the medium of radio. As with the 'Lovejoy Project' and auctioneering, the pupils of Exwick Middle school had a rare insight into a world of work, the commercial radio business, not generally available to young people.

Practical tasks

The main practical tasks were centred around History and English tasks, as well as communications and drama tasks.

- History and English tasks included the researching, collecting and collating of historical material, which included oral histories. Using the admissions register of the time and local contacts, the children wrote letters to individuals, articles for the local paper and made requests through radio and television for people who had gone to the school in 1938. To collect the information they sent out questionnaires and conducted interviews. They collated the results of the questionnaires and made a display of the photographs and artefacts handed in and sent to the school. Seventeen ex-pupils were invited to a reunion tea-party hosted by the children. The visitors were asked to recount their wartime experiences, which were recorded. Evidence was sifted by linking the oral stories with written evidence gleaned from the school log and through the local museum records (Exeter before and after the blitz). Each pupil kept a folder in which they wrote up their interviews alongside general information about the war period.
- Drama and communication tasks included learning the techniques of radio acting. The pupils began the process by recording a short scene, listening to their efforts, drawing out the weak points and trying again, to improve the quality. Through discussion, stories were selected and short scenes improvised. The most successful ones were then scripted in the format of a radio play. Trial cassette recordings were made and the final scenes were polished up. After much discussion, the final structure was agreed upon.
- The final rehearsal period involved trial recordings in school of the completed play with sound effects added. These recordings were listened to and evaluated before the recording of the play at Devon Air studios.

The significant event

In a studio at Devon Air in Exeter, two very nervous children were waiting for their cue to begin the recording of the radio drama 'I Wish I Was There'.

These two were supplying the important linking part of the drama, acting two naughty children of the present day who were in detention in the classroom for not doing the work set by their teacher. They did not know what to write so they began to wander around the classroom touching the World War II exhibits on display. They both started to read the school log and to imagine the incident recorded: the explosion of the school boiler. One of them said, 'I wish we were there' and suddenly they found themselves travelling back in time to the incident, watching it happen as if they were there! Finding themselves back in the classroom again, they thought they must have dreamt it. They move to another object in the display and touching it, one of them says, 'I wish we were there' again and once more they find themselves back in time witnessing the event of a severe flooding in the school.

After this second time they realize what is happening to them and so control the situation. They go back in time to four more incidents. When the teacher returns the children have started to write enthusiastically and are full of knowledge and excitement about the historical period around the time of World War II. The teacher is bemused, but the children keep their secret to themselves!

In 1992, two years after the event, those two 'naughty' children, now at secondary school, in commenting about the play had this to say:

> The experience was very good. We had never done anything like that before. It made learning fun. The play livened up the history which could be boring. We learnt about the war and we learnt about doing a radio play. It was worthwhile. I would do it again. (Lee Sanvitale)

> Being real, a lot was at stake. Because we were on the radio we knew we had to be good; lots of people were listening so I put a lot of effort into it. It was good with other people helping us as

well as our teachers and although at the beginning I thought that I wouldn't be able to stand up and do all that, I did manage to do it in the end and felt pleased and relieved. I'm sure that the confidence the play gave me has stayed with me. (Joanna Harris)

Example 5: 'buffet supper' by Montgomery Combined School

Résumé

This project is an example of integrating the cross-curricular theme of economic and industrial understanding into a food technology module taught to Year 7 pupils.

The buffet supper took place at the launch of the West Exe Business Education Partnership on 4 November 1992. The aim of the Partnership is to develop a productive relationship between education and business through a programme of initiatives designed to promote active business/education co-operation. It seemed very apt at such a launch to have a buffet that exemplified this partnership. The children, supported by Devon Direct Services, designed, prepared and served the buffet for the 100 invited guests from local businesses and the education authority.

Problem/question

The problem was a 'business/technical' one. How do we design, cost, arrange, prepare and serve a buffet supper for 100 people?

Interactive communication

In order for the children to have an active part in managing the buffet rather than just being told what to make and what to do, they needed to have an understanding of what was entailed in such an enterprise: what functions actually look like; what health and safety requirements were necessary in public functions; what organizing a buffet involved in relation to the food, i.e. cost, appearance, taste, suitability; the aesthetics of a buffet, i.e. arranging the tables, the decorations, the plates and serving dishes; and how caterers behaved at the actual functions when the guests arrived. These under-standings made the project a real experience of the catering business for the children as opposed to just learning the skills of cooking, the normal activity of this age group. The children were treated as full working partners in the enterprise with the success of the project based on their ability to feel that they could approach such an enterprise again with a more sophisticated understanding of requirements.

The attitudes and values nurtured by this approach included:

• a sense of responsibility for, and awareness of, the conse-quences of their own economic decisions;
• an interest in economic and industrial affairs;
• respect for the work of people in the catering business;
• recognizing the value of co-operative team approaches to tasks and problems;
• positive working relationships with adults other than their teachers;
• confidence in expressing creative ideas and showing initiat-ive; and
• sensitivity to the abilities, contribution and viewpoints of others.

Practical tasks

The tasks were undertaken by 15 Year 7 pupils in five morn-ing food technology sessions and from 3 p.m.–9.30 p.m. on Wednesday, 4 November 1992.

First, they identified the needs and opportunities, i.e. they:

• considered factors that needed to be taken into account in the planning, e.g. vegetarians, colour, cost, ease of prep-aration, restrictions of surroundings and dining circum-stances;
• used the expertize of the Devon County Caterers to get information about safety and advice on possible menus within the cost considerations; and

• worked out a suitable budget.

Second, they generated a design which involved:

• drawing up a list of possible items for inclusion in the menu;
• considering the criteria decided at the first stage, discarding unsuitable items; and
• choosing the final menu.

The children wrote the following.

> In choosing the menu we had to think about food that people could pick up with their fingers. They would be standing up so the food could not be difficult to eat. The food had to be cold. We had to think about how long it was going to take us. Cost was important too. The final OK list included: quiche, vol-au-vents, sausage rolls, sandwiches, cocktail sausages, cheese kebabs, cold meats, fruit cake, scones, chocolate truffles, pizza slices, fruit tartlets.

Third, they planned the event and made the food which involved:

• practising making the menu items in school, with help from Devon County Caterers;
• deciding on the table layout and decorations;
• deciding who would do what on the day; and
• preparing the food for the buffet.

Significant event

The buffet meal was a great success. From the interview with a group of the children one month after the event it is possible to discern the impact of the project on them. A number of aspects about the catering business had been learnt.

They understood the need for health and safety.

> There is a lot of difference between preparing food at home than for a buffet for 100 people because if you prepare for a buffet you have to take lots of precautions about what you wear.

Preparing food for lots of people, you have to take precautions like wearing hats. You have to make sure no germs get into the food so that no one gets food poisoning.

They understood the need to consider the customer.

We had to decide what would be easy to pick up with our fingers because it was a finger buffet so, for example, we thought chicken nuggets would be nice, and we had to think what they would like – not what we would like.

We did it for business people so they wouldn't like plastic plates, so we had to think of them. We are 11 and 12; we had to think of people a lot older than us.

I think the presentation was an important factor. If it is arranged nicely they think we would have taken care in preparing everything and there would be nothing wrong with the food.

They appreciated and understood the concept of costing. . . .

We didn't get paid but if we were working for a real business we would have to get paid. That would have added to the cost of the meal. So say if it was £1.84 for the food with the breakages and our wages it could be topped up to £3.50 a head.

Other things needed to be paid for like table mats, doileys, and napkins and the plates, although you could use the plates again . . .

. . . and value for money.

If we had charged £3.50 a head and the food was chucked on the table they would walk out – a waste of money!

They were now aware of some of the skills of being a caterer.

To be a caterer you need patience – there is a lot of waiting around . . . being a good cook . . . and being good at preparing things and setting things out . . . knowing all the rules . . . and being able to do things quickly on the day because you haven't got a lot of time.

You need to be good at costing things. You have got to buy all the ingredients, allow for breakages and everything so it is hard to know how much profit you are going to make. As it is hard to know how much profit margin you can allow for it really needs to be well thought out and planned before you start.

And finally, they experienced a real sense of satisfaction and achievement.

On the day we had one or two compliments from each person – saying it was arranged nicely and we must have taken care and who prepared this and that and it tasted nice. We all felt quite proud really . . .

. . . we wanted some congratulations for it . . .

. . . yes, it took us about six to eight hours to prepare it all.

Yes, we would do it again. I think we would be able to do it quite easily because we have had the experience now. So if you need that kind of thing done again you can come to 'Montgomery Enterprises'.

Concluding comment

This chapter has sought to show, through actual examples of practice, the lively and enriching way that cross-curricular activities can be incorporated in an integrated way into the primary school curriculum. These particular projects have one special attribute in common: the pupils were central to the proceedings. They became the owners of work that was exposed to outside scrutiny; they all 'rose' to the events, displaying remarkable social skills beyond the expectations of their teachers. Without fail all the teachers alluded to the exemplary behaviour and 'mature' attitudes of the children. Remember these children range from 7 to 12 years. How many adults could cope with giving a speech in front of dignitaries, subjecting their food preparation to business executives, performing in front of a live audience in a London theatre, auctioneering before an audience of 200 people and taking part in a professional radio play that went out on the commercial air waves?

These kinds of real-life experiences do not fit neatly into the National Curriculum statement of attainments and programmes of study. Such a system gives minimal credit to the complex and inter-related achievements individually experienced by each and every child. This comment by one of the headteachers sums up the feelings of all when reviewing the value of cross-curricular work.

In the overall education of the children we must be careful not to be governed and constrained by the rather tight parameters of what children have to learn for the National Curriculum. There is something about doing this kind of cross-curricular work that has value in its own right and if it touches the National curriculum then well and good. But the experiences the children have is not written up anywhere in the National Curriculum. The value of it is difficult to get hold of but it is part of school experience. It is exciting. It touches the emotions and is the feeling of, 'I have done something excellent in my life and I am proud of the achievement'. Unless we push these frontiers we are going to stay in a mundane world and never risk something and all of us need a risk in our lives somewhere. That is what sets the adrenalin going and pushes the boundaries out. There is a place for this in its own right without even getting the National Curriculum documents out of the cupboard.

Chapter 4

CROSS-CURRICULAR
ELEMENTS: SECONDARY
PRACTICE

Chapter 3 showed how the primary sector of education could accommodate cross-curricular activities into its present organizational structures. The primary classroom with one teacher managing the learning for a group of students throughout their school day is a conducive environment for integrating differing subject matter in a meaningful way, but the situation in the secondary school is more complex. The core of the secondary school curriculum is subject teaching. The vast majority of the resource allocation is divided up between the subjects and every member of staff (and this includes deputy heads), regardless of other responsibilities, is assigned to a subject area.

Since the 1988 Education Reform Act, the secondary school curriculum has been in a constant state of dynamic change. Ask any National Curriculum subject teacher and s/he will tell you about 'innovation overload'. i.e. experience of having to put new teaching programmes into practice in a very short space of time. One Head of Science in a secondary school reports that he has begun each school year from 1988 onwards unable to teach the same programme of study as the previous year because of externally imposed changes. He cites two examples of recent changes in science education: first, the National Curriculum Science Orders originally had 17 attainment targets, which were then reduced to 4; and second, the change from single sciences to double science at GCSE was made in order to accommodate all three sciences of physics, chemistry and biology into the time allocation at GCSE level (Key Stage 4).

If the teachers' day-to-day existence is dominated by the restructuring of their teaching programme and assessment activities for the statutory curriculum, there will have been little time to review, consider carefully and reflect on the implementation of the non-statutory curriculum, of which the cross-curricular themes are a central part. This view is endorsed by a recent research study funded by the Economic and Social Research Council, whose researchers, Gabrielle Rowe and Geoff Whitty, claim that

> whatever curriculum audits showed, the themes had a rather shadowy presence in most of the schools that we visited. It is difficult to see how they will recover from the present situation when so much emphasis is placed on the subject orders. (*TES*, 9 April 1993)

However, it is also the case that the cross-curriculum elements in place before the 1988 Act have been retained by schools during the changes in the subject curriculum. These include PSE programmes in tutor time, IT, the work experience aspect of EIU through the TVEI-funded programme and careers education for 16-year-old students to help them decide on further education, training or employment.

What many schools have been developing over the last year or two is the realignment of on-going practice in the area of cross-curricular elements with the new NCC guidelines, as described in Chapter 2. As they have come to terms with the basic structure of the National Curriculum they are beginning to tackle the issue of the whole curriculum and to examine in more detail the inclusion of the cross-curricular themes of health, environment, citizenship, economic and industrial understanding and careers education and guidance. Many schools have appointed a cross-curricular co-ordinator to carry out this task. A popular way to begin this process is by engaging in the activity of curriculum mapping. One cross-curricular co-ordinator in a comprehensive school of 1000 pupils, interviewed on 8 July 1993, describes the process:

> What I needed to do initially and what I have done is to map the curriculum. Mapping was not free of problems because with so

many changes it was partly out of date as quickly as I could do it! People moved, syllabuses changed, working practices changed, new bits of National Curriculum arrived but it has given me a starting point. It needed a lot of time. I delved through all the information I could find out and picked out the main points within each theme and asked the teachers through a questionnaire what they felt they did. I coded every one of those responses and mapped it all on a huge chart which had every member of staff on it. This roughly informed us where I thought we were.

This mapping exercise is fairly common practice amongst cross-curricular co-ordinators. It gives them a picture of present practice and through this process of identification they can plan for the future in a systematic way, offering realistic suggestions of how to approach the incorporation of a full range of the cross-curricular elements into their respective schools. In the same way that the organization of the teaching of the curriculum is decided by the school management team so too is the organization of cross-curricular work. Different approaches are being trialled in many schools as they seek to find suitable ways to implement cross-curricular elements. This process of development is active and on-going within the present climate of change.

Coping with curriculum development in cross-curricular work is as important for student teachers entering the profession as it is for practising teachers. Indeed, the teaching profession needs new teachers to be actively aware of their responsibility to engage in these activities, so this is one area where teacher educators, student teachers and school teachers should work in partnership to develop curriculum practices that relate aspects of the cross-curricular themes to the subject-based secondary curriculum. The School of Education at the University of Exeter has focused on cross-curricular work as a key strand in the educational studies component of the undergraduate course for trainee secondary school teachers: first, the course familiarizes the students with the knowledge areas of the cross-curricular themes and gives them the opportunity to investigate the way these specific themes interrelate with their respective subject disciplines; second, it enables them to put this knowledge into practice by developing, piloting and reviewing a cross-curricular teaching project of their own devising, for a specific class in a local school – Westlands School in Torquay; and third, it equips them to participate in the cross-curricular development work taking place in the school during their final 10-week teaching practice. This course provides a rich source of information about developments and practice across a range of secondary schools, with students on teaching practice in schools in Cornwall, Devon, Dorset, Somerset and London. This chapter will give insights into the variety of approaches schools are adopting via the perspectives and the development work of some of these student teachers. Usually, only a selection of hypothetical possibilities of practice are available through published in-service resource packs. Here, we offer first-hand reports of what is actually happening in the schools.

Approaches to cross-curricular work

Four ways of organizing cross-curricular work within the school curriculum are identifiable at this time.

1. *The special event approach*   The whole school or one section within the school like a year group focus on a particular area, for example an 'environment week' or a 'health week'.
2. *Particular timetabled slot*   Cross-curricular themes are part of a separate PSE programme and are dealt within a lesson slot allocated in the week, e.g. lessons about careers.
3. *Subject connection*   Specific subjects take ownership of a theme, e.g. religious education and citizenship, PE and health.
4. *Subject and theme integration*   The subjects try to cover aspects of any one of the themes in their lessons where appropriate, i.e. mathematics teachers try to include 'environment' as much as the geography teacher does.

A combination of some of these approaches are possible within one school but for the purposes of illuminating examples of practice each approach will be taken in turn.

The special event

Towards the end of the summer term many schools have traditionally held an activities week, particularly for Years 7, 8 and 9 (11–14 yr-olds). The normal timetable is reconstructed and the school students participate in different events organized and run by members of staff. In order to stimulate interest and involvement in the cross-curricular themes some schools have taken this generally accepted practice and given it a thematic emphasis. Two examples follow which indicate the way such thematic special events work.

Health week at an Avon school

In this school, the PE department had received from the headteacher the NCC guidelines on health education (NCC 1990c) but at their department meeting they decided that health education was a whole-school concern. As a department they agreed to take up a suggestion made by one (a former student of the School of Education, Exeter University) for a 'health week' and to involve as many other departments in the school as could be persuaded to contribute to the week. This idea was put to the headteacher, who gave his support, so the Head of PE presented the idea at a faculty meeting where general support was given. The PE department then took responsibility for shaping and developing the idea. It was decided to have a week in June for Years 7, 8 and 9 and to include involvement from outsiders as well as the non-teaching support services in the school – the canteen staff, the librarian and the school nurse. The week before the event, booklets were circulated to the pupils and the staff to give them a general overview.

The introduction in the pupil booklet indicated the general tone of the week.

The aim of the Health Week is to encourage you to:
1. think about what it means 'to be healthy' in detail;

2. consider carefully whether *you* lead a healthy lifestyle; and
3. decide on realistic steps you are going to take, which will improve your level of health and your enjoyment in the future.

THINK! Are you healthy?
Fifty years ago, people thought of 'health' as simply being 'free from illness'. Today, however, we have begun to realize that being healthy is far more than just a 'physical' thing, rather it involves our whole body and mind. What does the word health mean to you? If an alien came up and asked you to explain what it means 'to be healthy' what would you say? Share your ideas with those around you.
Years 7, 8 and 9 will be considering 'health' in more detail as the week goes on.

1. First, you will consider health through your subject lessons. Some departments have decided to consider one specific aspect of health but the majority of subjects have chosen to look at a variety of interpretations of the word 'health'. You will be thinking and discussing a large range of issues over the week and hopefully, by listening carefully and sharing ideas, your knowledge and understanding of the word 'health' will increase.
2. Second, throughout the whole week many activities and opportunities will be available to you to find out more about different aspects of health and to get involved on 'healthy' activities in your lunchtimes and after school. Look at the itinerary for the week to find out exactly what is going on. There is something for everyone! Not just sports that make you hot and sweaty!

The timetable was not abandoned as such, but the health-based curriculum was wrapped around it with the subject-based curriculum dealing with health issues. Lunchtimes and after-school time were filled with activities that ranged from talks about drinking and driving by the police to sessions in Aikido and the Alexander Technique.

Each subject area took a particular approach in lesson time. Science lessons centred around the adverse effects of smoking, advertising, and an anti-smoking campaign for Year 7 and Year 8 pupils plus a topic on what diseases can be avoided by being more healthy. In English lessons, the pupils discussed the promotion (or disguising) of healthy images through

77

advertising and wrote about the utilization of leisure time and holidays.

Learning vocabulary concerning food, diet and healthy recipes was concentrated on in the foreign language lessons, whereas in the religious education lessons the pupils discussed in what way religious belief helped towards spiritual health. Food was also the topic chosen by the art department, where pupils designed and produced visual health displays. The PE department concentrated on fitness, and new activities were offered both in lesson time and after school. The library displayed books on health and the canteen offered healthy alternative food, introducing a salad bar and jacket potatoes to break the habit of chips with everything.

Environment days at a south Devon school

This event grew out of the matrix teams at the school. Every member of staff is part of a cross-curricular team of teachers who meet regularly four times a term to discuss ways of incorporating cross-curricular elements into the curriculum planning and classroom teaching. The matrix team structure is designed so that the different subject areas are represented in each team.

Last academic year, the environment team were concerned that the take-up of environmental issues within subjects was very limited so they suggested that the school should mount three environmental days for Years 7, 8 and 9 (while year 10 was on work experience and Year 11 would have left following their GCSE examinations) to 'kick start' staff into developing environmental curriculum resources. The regular timetable was disbanded but pupils remained in their normal teaching groups and participated in half-day learning sessions that focused on environmental issues devised by the different subjects areas of technology, English, science, mathematics, expressive arts and modern languages.

One activity in English is a typical example of those set up for Year 9 pupils. It focused on written and oral communication skills within the context of an environmental improvement project. The teacher set the activity up and discussed procedures, and then the pupils went out of school to the site of the project where they collected the information needed to carry out the task. The session began in school with pupils being issued the following memo.

TEIGNBRIDGE DISTRICT COUNCIL
Council Maintenance Department
Memo

From: Council Property Maintenance Manager
To: Council Property Inspectors

At the recent meeting of Teignbridge Council Property Managers, a plan to award an improvement grant to the estate known as Broadlands was unanimously approved.

An improvement building programme will be drawn up and implemented in the autumn. The first step involves you as property inspectors. We require you to inspect the estate and to recommend what should be improved with the grant money.

Your task today is to produce:

1. a description of the condition of the estate; and
2. a list of recommendations for improvement in priority order.

The chair of the environment matrix team evaluated the three-day event and wrote a report. Her concluding comment is given here.

Were the days successful? How do we measure success? These following lines seem to give a theme to the evaluation of the three days:

> I say: take no thought of the harvest,
> But only of proper sowing.
> (T. S. Eliot, Choruses from *The Rock*, reproduced by permission, Faber and Faber Ltd)

The seeds have been sown in every curriculum area and the responses from the curriculum areas show that many good seeds were skilfully sown. Of the actual harvest I can make no comment for it is the pupils of Years 7, 8 and 9 who are to be the reapers. In these three days we were working for the long-term future, ensuring, as well as we were able, the proper sowing. We need to continue to nurture the seeds but the harvest will inevitably be for the children to reap.

79

Particular timetabled PSE slot

From a pupil's perspective, the academic subject-based curriculum of the secondary school means meeting a lot of different teachers in different classrooms in any one day. To help the pupil cope with this curriculum organization schools have evolved pastoral structures, which are their way of giving each child a sense of belonging within the school community. There are various patterns of pastoral organization but they all share the notion of a personal tutor. Every child is assigned to a teacher whose role as tutor includes taking responsibility for the overall development of the child as s/he goes through the school. The tutor will keep a file of all information pertinent to that child, on-going records of achievement, school reports, information about the child's primary education and knowledge about the child's background. It is in the role of tutor that traditionally the secondary teacher has been predominantly concerned with the personal development and the social welfare of the child. To complement this pastoral support, a number of schools also offer a period of time set aside on the timetable for developing personal skills and raising social awareness. Cross-curricular themes appear within these PSE programmes because they are recognized as being centrally concerned with the personal and social education of young people. David Brown, a student teacher on teaching practice, noted with interest the way that the cross-curricular activities in both the tutor time and the PSE programme in his teaching practice school in Dorset was augmented by the positive use of the school assembly as a medium for complementary cross-curricular work.

> This school adheres to the practice of using assembly time for delivering not just school news but also social and moral issues. This was emphasized and there was consistently a cross-curricular theme addressed in almost every assembly that I witnessed. The pastoral care system can be seen as the *raison d'être* of the year assembly; principally it is the allotted time where the heads of year concern themselves more specifically with issues which arise concerning their year group. Issues that I observed covered such topics as bullying, both physical and psychological, getting involved

in school life and extra-curricular activities, classroom behaviour, discipline both self and in a group. In each case the assembly concerned itself with contemporary incidents rather than an arbitrary topic.

In contrast, the twice-weekly lower school assemblies (Years 7, 8 and 9 together) presented broader themes and issues. The assembly can be seen as a very particular kind of learning environment, a brief but powerful medium, raising issues of a personal, social, moral and environmental nature. Assemblies can be used to offer reflective and factual observations of the real world outside of school. One of the Deputy Heads on reflecting on his approach to upper/lower school assemblies stated:

> This an injection of a bit of, maybe unpleasant, adult reality into the children's world . . . what we are doing is imposing some kind of responsibility and adult, mature behaviour at the beginning of the day where we are saying: 'Yes, great. Life can be fun, but think about this.' (interview transcript, 3 March 1993)

Due to the brevity of the assembly, the concentration span for pupils is unproblematic; the main factor is to acquire the attention of the pupils. One occasion in particular demonstrated how pupils' interest and attention were captured. In this assembly, two upper-school pupils performed an interesting and arresting narrative. The topic was the two faces of tourism in Thailand and India. The pupils were presented with two different perspectives: on the one hand, the glossy advertizing campaigns of the tourist industry; and on the other the reality of countless cases of secret torture and murder of innocent people by the authorities of these countries. The two sides were played off against each other, sentence by sentence. It was very simple and yet very effective. The two senior pupils doing the presentation belong to a group of committed young people at the school concerned with human rights issues; they used information from Amnesty International as a way of alerting the pupils to the value of the work of such a voluntary organization. The involvement of older pupils made this issue more accessible to younger pupils and also showed them how individuals can give expression of their concern about human rights through being part of an organization that has an international network.

Subject connection

Both approaches to cross-curricular work described so far are important facets of the general school life; they help to link young people to the world around them. In the case of the special events, pupils became more aware of the facilities available to them and the environment in which they live, while the PSE work gives them a time in each week where the learning is pupil-centred. However, these activities may leave the day-to-day life and learning in the classroom virtually untouched by considerations of the cross-curricular themes; thus they remain as a 'shadowy presence'. As discussed in Chapter 2 each theme contains a number of coherent concepts and direct links exist between some of these and the concepts inherent within the core and foundation subjects of the National Curriculum. Pupils can be encouraged to utilize the subject knowledge taught together with their personal knowledge and, in a practical way, grapple with real-life issues, solving everyday problems. Then the subject knowledge takes on a new relevance for the pupils. Curriculum planning takes on an extra dimension when attempts are made to achieve some balance between the prescribed subject attainment targets and the knowledge constructs that make up the cross-curricular themes. Some links are more obvious than others; these can be more readily incorporated into subject programmes, and so some subjects can take on certain aspects of some of the themes with relative ease. The two examples of practical lessons that follow, devised and taught by student teachers in Westlands School, illustrate this. Each lesson lasted for one hour.

Example 1: The teaching of environment within the geography National Curriculum

These two lessons were taught to an all-ability Year 10 group of pupils with emphasis on discussion, group work and giving pupils the opportunity to develop and articulate their views on the environmental issues attached to the more factual knowledge they had acquired with regard to rainforests.

The *aim* of the lesson was to create an awareness about the environmental factors connected with the rainforest and to recognize the implications to the world at large.

During the first lesson, the pupils were given world maps and introduced to the idea of rainforests: what they are and where they are. Three words were then written on the board: LOCATION CLIMATE SOIL. Pupils were asked to work on their own and to write down, for each heading, their importance to the rainforest. A class discussion to collate their ideas, written on the board, led on to class responses to the following questions:

- Why are there large gaps in the bands of rainforests?
- What does the population map tell you about the rainforest regions?
- Do any industrialized countries have rainforests?

Then the class were given a worksheet with statements on it that were either true or false. They watched an educational video about the rainforest and then completed the worksheet. Again, their answers were discussed as a whole-class activity. In pairs, they discussed reasons for the loss of rainforests, their ideas were considered by the whole class and written on the board. The next part of the video was watched after which, in groups of three, they prepared an interview that was videoed the following week. Each group comprised an interviewer, one person giving the case of the local inhabitants against the destruction of the rainforest and one person giving the government's case for using the rainforest as a natural resource of government finance. The pupils had literature available to make their cases.

In the follow-up lesson, the prepared interviews were videoed and after watching them the class had a plenary discussion centred around four questions:

- Why should the rainforests be cut down?
- Why should the rainforests *not* be cut down?
- What do you think should happen to the rainforests?

- Why is the issue of the rainforests so important to the world at large?

In evaluating the lessons, the student teachers noted a high level of pupils' understanding about the environmental issues evidenced by the quality of the video interviews and the plenary discussion.

Example 2: education for EIU through mathematics

This lesson was designed for a Year 8 group of children described as slow learners. Active learning through group work (with teacher support) was the predominant strategy employed, followed by discussion to share understandings gained in the lesson.

The *aim* of the lesson was to develop pupil awareness of themselves as consumers in the market-place. This was relevant to aspects of the Mathematics curriculum: Using and applying mathematics and Handling data, together with NC Guidance 4 (*EIU*: Companies compete in business through innovation, price, advertizing, aiming to increase their share of the market and sell more goods and services).

The pupils formed groups to represent a family and were given the task of buying the food for one week for a family of four. They were given a map, showing the sites of the available shops: a supermarket, a small store and a corner shop. The pupils were provided with a list of items to buy and the prices of these items in the various shops. Each group was assigned a house where they lived, and the map indicated the distance between their homes and the various shops. They were told that travelling costs to the shops amounted to 10p per kilometre. They were then encouraged to shop daily and each day, when the pupils arrived at the various shops, they were given notice of available offers.

During the lesson, the 'buying' took place for the whole week and the total cost of the shopping was calculated in each group. The class then discussed the different problems and aspects that arose during the activity, and who managed to get the best buys, which group spent the least, and which the most. The pupils were finally asked to consider what they had learnt from the activity.

In evaluating the lesson, the student teachers discovered that the pupils had realized the importance of 'shopping around' to make the most of their limited money. They also realized that shopkeepers employed different strategies to induce customers to buy their goods – but not always to the customer's advantage. They had experienced being a consumer and had begun to ask questions, and find their own answers, as to why supermarkets could undercut the corner shop.

Subject and theme integration

The lesson content in the two examples just given was very different, but there were similarities: through connecting a theme to a subject they brought real-life social issues into the classroom; and both actively engaged pupils in a task that asked them to reach decisions. Here we have practical examples of relevance in the educational context. The children used their own personal knowledge i.e. what they know and bring to the lesson, including factual information, attitudes they hold and skills they have; this is demonstrated by the way they work with, and communicate to, others. This co-operation with others is positively built into the lesson through group work, and the communication skill is required and used in the structured discussions, either in small groups and with the whole class. To this, they add their subject knowledge pertinent to the lesson, i.e. the public knowledge they all share (the geographical knowledge about what a rainforest is or mathematical knowledge about how to calculate money and distance). So, both lessons demonstrated a particular teaching and learning structure where the pupils are expected to draw on their personal knowledge and to utilize their skills in a creative, individual and practical way whilst at the same time learning new, and applying already acquired, subject knowledge. This is possible because the cross-curricular themes deal with social knowledge, inherent in both geography and mathematics, i.e. the need to pay attention to attitudes and values. The NCC (NCC, 1990a, p. 6) makes this point.

> The themes have in common the ability to foster discussion of questions of value and belief; they add to knowledge and understanding and they rely on practical activities, decision making and the interrelationship of the individual and the community.

The attitudes and values held by individuals are acquired through socialization. Education within school is part of this socialization process and the cross-curricular themes tackle this personal dimension head on. Across the five themes, key notions about the kinds of attitude and values that young people should hold in a democratic and morally decent society appear: independence, responsibility, respect, concern, choice and appreciation. The nurturing of such attributes requires a conducive social context, and since the classroom is part of that social context, it has to be consistent in its working relationships – teacher-pupil and pupil-pupil – with these personal and social qualities. Therefore the medium (the how) of learning in the classroom is just as important as the ideas, information and skills (the what) that are being learnt. Paying heed to the cross-curricular themes within subject lessons therefore provides the teacher with a manageable structure with which to incorporate practical, personal and productive learning in an integrated and relevant way, with the subject knowledge thus enriching classroom learning experiences.

In terms of content too, it is possible to see each theme as not being mutually exclusive. A study of the components of each theme show linkages. For example, citizenship, being so broadly conceptualized, could encompass aspects of all the others. There are eight essential components to this theme: the nature of community; roles and relationships in a pluralistic society; the duties, responsibilities and rights of being a citizen; the family, democracy in action; the citizen and law; work, employment and leisure; and the public services. An obvious link with citizenship is health education, since they both cover family life and hence safety and sex education.

EIU links with the community component in citizenship which deals with finance and industry which in turn relates to work, employment and leisure, and hence careers. Finally environment has natural links with citizenship through democracy in action and human rights, whilst also being crucial to health education and the world of work – EIU and careers. This awareness of the inter-connectedness of the themes can be quite liberating; it is possible to consider creative, challenging and novel ways to make subject knowledge more meaningful to the children, by electing to give them a different perspective and thus a fresh look at both the subject content and the thematic social issues. Five examples follow of subject lessons that integrate the themes in this way. The student teachers found that in planning the lessons, remaining true to the spirit of the cross-curricular aims of building on personal knowledge, raising social issues and taking heed, in a positive way, of attitudes and values meant that the lessons included at the very least:

- practical tasks;
- group work; and
- group and/or class discussion of ideas and opinions.

All the lessons were concerned with fostering:

- independence of though;
- tolerance and open-mindedness;
- respect for the beliefs and opinions of others; and
- concern and appreciation of democratic decision-making.

Consequently, communication skills are always present and the equal opportunities dimension permeates the very structure of the lessons. Also, of course, none of these lessons are perfect, since they have been devised by student teachers and trialled in classrooms unknown to the students prior to the curriculum development project. However, they do show challenging and interesting learning experiences, and these give a hint of the enriching possibilities for schools who are seriously trying to integrate subjects and themes into the day-to-day life of classrooms. The subject references in each example relate to the National Curriculum Orders that pre-date the most recent 1994 version.

Example 1: Health in a French lesson

This lesson was designed for a Year 10 class that found French difficult. The *aim* of the lesson was to introduce pupils to the concept of a balanced diet using French as a medium. The relevant subject reference was Reading; understand and respond to short factual texts and non-factual texts, both printed and handwritten, which include sentences containing short clauses and some unfamiliar language; deduce the meaning of unfamiliar words using knowledge of language and script alongside NCC (1990c) Guidance 5 (*Health Education*: Food and nutrition – know that individual health requires a varied diet).

During the lesson the pupils began by responding, as a class, to questions (in English) about food – what they liked, or didn't like – leading to the question: What is a balanced diet? Their initial thoughts were pooled and recorded on the blackboard. They were then given a French text about food and nutrition to translate into English. They worked in pairs helping each other, with the aid of a dictionary. The translated text then acted as the basis for teacher input about the seven components of a balanced diet. A team quiz followed, called 'Diet Knowledge', in which the pupils had the chance, in an enjoyable and relaxed way, to check out their knowledge about nutrition. This led to group work in which the pupils suggested what might be considered a balanced diet in England and in France, discussing the cultural differences and learning the French terms for various foods.

In evaluating the lesson it was noted the pupils had enjoyed learning new French words. In the discussions they had voiced opinions about the food they ate, which resulted in a raised awareness about the cultural and lifestyle differences between the two countries. They also recognized the influence that being part of the European community was having on the eating habits of themselves and their families.

Example 2: Thinking about careers in PE

These two lessons took place with a Year 10 group who were studying PE as a GCSE subject. The lesson worked at two levels: the pupils were involved in experiential learning by both participating in the acquisition of skills and engaging in the processes of teaching these skills; and it also extended into discussion about careers with PE and sport.

The *aims* of the lesson were to:

- give the pupils an insight into the role of a PE teacher;
- extend the pupil's knowledge of careers in PE and sport;
- develop interaction through group discussion; and
- increase their skill level at basketball.

The relevant NC references were PE PoS leading to the end of Key Stage 4 (Pupils should be aware of social issues associated with the activities undertaken, and pupils should be helped to understand the importance of the roles of responsible participants) and NCC (1990d) Guidance 6 (*Careers Education and Guidance*: to be aware of education training and career opportunities).

During the first lesson, the pupils were involved in two main activities: one active, and the other, discursive and reflective. For the first activity, the class was divided into five groups of four. There were five skills to be covered with a task card for each, and five skill stations were therefore set up in the gym. One member of each group took on the role of teacher and organized the others in the group to increase their basketball skills. A time limit was set for each skill station and the groups rotated in turn. After a slow start – not having worked in this way before – the class began to take responsibility for the activity and work their way through the five skills. After the active part of the lesson, the pupils were asked to reflect on what they had learnt. They talked about how they had had to organize themselves and the skills a teacher needs to be able to explain, coach and help others to improve their skill levels in a given sport.

This discussion led into the follow-up lesson where the same groups were asked to elect a spokesperson and to respond to the following four questions.

* How many jobs can you think of associated with PE and sport?
* What do you think might be the qualifications required for these jobs?
* What do you think is the difference between a PE teacher and a coach?
* What are the qualities of a good teacher?

Each spokesperson gave feedback to the whole class and the main ideas were written on the blackboard. The lesson ended with an informal quiz that was team-based. The questions referred to what had been highlighted and the children could remember quite a lot. The pupils found the lessons interesting and relevant and had enjoyed co-operating together.

In evaluating the lesson it was clear that the pupils had gained some insight into the role of the teacher through experiencing it themselves. They learnt some new skills, had engaged in purposeful talk and were more aware about career opportunities in PE and sport than before.

Example 3: Citizenship through technology

This lesson was devised for Year 7 pupils perceived as slow learners. The juxtaposition of the theme of citizenship with technology was a challenging one and as the technology lesson was using the medium of textiles, the lesson centred on clothing.

The *aim* of the lesson was to investigate the notion of stereotyping, through pupil's response to the clothes people wear, and independence of thought on moral and social issues, and the appreciation that personal experience may influence changes in an individual's values and beliefs.

The relevant subject references were Identifying needs and

opportunities and Organizing and planning alongside NCC (1990f) Guidance 8 (*Citizenship*: Aspects of the community component).

During the lesson, the pupils were engaged in three activities that developed communication skills: an oral and written activity, role-play and group discussion. In the first activity, each group was given a pack of cards, each card describing a particular life role – tramp, teacher, pop star, etc. – and in their groups they were asked to list the clothes that they would expect a person of that type to wear without indicating to whom they were referring. After five minutes, the sheets were rotated and the groups were then asked to identify the characteristics of the life role of the person they would associate with each of these sets of clothes. The groups then shared their deliberations, looking to see if the characteristics identified by one group matched the initial card or not. Some turned out to be the same as the card and others did not. The class decided that it was easy to match when the clothes matched a general expectation, i.e. when the stereotypical image was strong.

For the second activity, the pupils were asked, in groups, to act out a short scene that contained a particular individual displaying characteristics that could be expected of that individual, e.g. a nurse. However, there were certain words that they were not allowed to use, e.g. for the nurse these would be nurse, hospital, ward, injection, etc. The role plays were short – about a minute – and the rest of the class had to guess the identity of the main character. The notion of stereotype was discussed, and the strength of the stereotype relative to the speed of the guessing.

The third activity linked the issue of stereotyping to textiles, by exploring more generally the clothes people wore. The class discussion led to three main points being formulated when choosing or designing clothes: personal choice; comfort and practicality; and the impression the clothes would convey to others.

In evaluating the lesson the student teachers noted that the pupils were quick to recognize the judgements and stereotypes made in each of the activities and they felt that the pupils had been made conscious of these through being engaged in active learning. A number of pupils commented at the end of the lesson that it had been a very different lesson from the usual and it had made them think differently about clothes. In summary, it was generally felt that it was wrong to judge someone by the clothes they wear rather than personal merits. However, although they did not wish to be judged that way, they felt that often they would be, and in order to get on in life they probably would have to compromise between their individual wants and other people's expectations.

Example 4: Environment education through English

This lesson shows how the skills of English for communication are practised in a non-literary lesson that has, as its content, a current environmental issue. The lessons were taught to Year 7 high achievers.

The *aims* of the lesson were to explore language use through studying the writing in two different English newspapers, and to arouse pupils' awareness about the environment and the impact that humans can have on it.

The relevant NC references are AT2 (Reading: 6(c) show in discussion that they recognize whether subject matter in non-literary text and media text is fact or opinion, identifying some of the ways in which the distinction can be made), AT3 (Writing: 5(e) show in discussion the ability to recognize variations in vocabulary according to purpose, topic and audience and whether language is spoken or written and use them appropriately in writing, AT4/5 (Presentation: 6(d) show some ability to use any available presentational devices that are appropriate to the task so that finished work is presented clearly and attractively, and NCC (1990e) Guidance 7 (*Environmental Education*: The interaction between human activities and the environment).

During the lesson the pupils were introduced to two different newspapers – a tabloid and a broadsheet – and asked to comment on the different styles of these papers and the use of language. Questions were asked about whether the pupils read a newspaper or not and, if they did so, which one and what they liked to read. After the general introduction, the student teachers asked them to focus on the reports of the *Braer* disaster (the oil tanker that ran aground in Quendale Bay in the Shetlands on 5 January 1993). The pupils split into groups of two or three and studied the accounts of the disaster in the newspapers provided. Then the class came together to consider the information gleaned, the pooled ideas being written on the board. This led into a discussion on the differences in presentation between the two papers. The pupils were very observant and came up with differences that covered style of writing content and type of language used. They were then given another task. The class was divided into four groups each given an environmental focus: people, scenery, economy and wildlife. They were asked to write sections of text relevant to their focus and suitable for either a tabloid or broadsheet newspaper. In the follow-up lesson they completed a front page with a headline and a story in the newspaper style of their choice. They worked very hard to produce the final versions.

In evaluating the lessons the student teachers felt that they had gone some way to meeting their aims. The pupils had worked individually (when they were reading the articles and writing their own), as a whole class (when discussing the issues) and in small mixed set groups (when producing the front page). There had been an opportunity for pupils to express their opinions and to acquire new information as well as using a number of English skills in the context of the environment. The pupils said that they had learnt much about the effect of the oil spillage on that environment.

Example 5: EIU through science
In the National Curriculum revised orders the applications and economic, social and technological implications of science are included in the programmes of study (PoS) that support the four attainment targets (ATs) in science. This lesson was devised for a double-award GCSE science group in Year 10.

The *aim* of the lesson was to develop pupils' knowledge and understanding of the economic functioning of the world by focusing on advances in technology made through scientific discoveries.

The relevant NC references: were at Key Stage 4 (Pupils should develop their knowledge and understanding of the ways in which scientific ideas change through time and how the nature of these ideas and the uses to which they are put are affected by the social, moral, spiritual and cultural contexts in which they are developed; in doing so they should begin to recognize that while science is an important way of thinking about experience, it is not the only way) and NCC (1990b) Guidance 4 (*Education for EIU*: Component of industry and work and the economic concepts of supply and demand).

During the lesson, the pupils participated in a role-play simulation, the 'Car Design Game'. The class was split into six groups, a car design team for each of the following countries: USA, France, Brazil, India, Kenya and Ghana. The task was for each team to design a car within a pre-specified budget that would be marketable, safe, environmentally friendly and economic. Each team had the available design options for cars and the prices for each of these options (relative to the economic and technological advancement of that country). The director of the multi-national car manufacturing company (the teacher!) was holding a conference at which the car design teams were invited to 'sell' their designs after which the contract would be awarded to one of the six teams. So, in the lesson, the pupils had to do two things: decide how best to spend their budget and come up with a design; and then work out their sales pitch for the director and be ready to respond to questions from the director and other conference members.

In evaluating the lesson, the majority of the comments from the pupils were about the realization, through the experience of being put in that position, of the predominance of economic considerations in the world market-place. The teacher's evaluation was that this lesson could be used in a modified version at the end of a project to see whether a scientific discovery is marketable. In fact, the greater the knowledge base about the product or discovery that the children have then the more successful the simulation would be.

Concluding comments

These four approaches have been exemplified, separately, to illustrate the contribution of each one towards providing a broad, balanced and relevant curriculum for all. To conclude this chapter, a school's present practice in implementing a mixture of these approaches is presented as viewed by a 1993 graduate student teacher.

A case study of practice in a South Devon community college, reported by Bruce Butt

In the ten weeks spent on teaching practice at this community college, I saw an encouraging and forward-thinking example of positive practice of the many ways in which cross-curricular themes may be incorporated into a school's curriculum. One member of staff was appointed to research how a new programme might be developed, and teamed up with the co-ordinator of the already established PSME programme. It was felt that the way the themes were taught was crucial and had to incorporate pupils thinking critically about the issues – asking questions, being presented with different points of view etc. – and that this was inextricably linked with their personal, social and moral thinking, hence connected with PSME programme. It was recognized that a totally radical review involving every aspect of the timetable would not be feasible due to other curriculum commitments. Therefore those areas already covered, such as environmental education in geography and science, were left unchanged – although further supplementation might well occur in the curriculum. As the cross-curricular co-ordinator said, '. . . there is something a little chancy and limiting about isolating cross-curricular work to 'community studies' or tutorial work or any single area alone.'

The following are typical examples of the way the themes were implemented within the school.

- The tutor period had a defined and prescribed programme, and the assemblies were built into this programme.
- Pupils in Year 9 in their geography subject lessons were involved in National Tree-planting Week, attending to a piece of woodland.

- Current events were used as a device within Year 8 for linking information technology and media studies in English to scrutinize media coverage and produce their own paper.
- Information technology, as well as existing in its own right as a subject, in Years 7 and 8, was also a medium for other subjects such as mathematics, geography as well as the example already cited in English.
- Design technology also featured a strong cross-themes presence through, arguably, a PSME perspective, as the school took part in a 'Neighbourhood Engineers' scheme where people with experience in the engineering industry came into school and worked co-operatively with the teachers.
- Physical Education also had community links drawing from expertise in local sports clubs and participating in company-sponsored courses therefore adding the themes of citizenship and health education to their programmes of study.
- Economic and industrial understanding was seen in a particular form when upper-school pupils made, marketed and sold their own products as a 'small business'. This was complemented by a work experience with pupils going for a fortnight to banks, shops, sports centres, offices as well as to work in businesses particular to the area – tourist work, hotels, boat building and farm placements.

Although, at the school's own admission, the practice demonstrated in the school had its weak points, I believe a comprehensive and imaginative cross-curricular base has been established in a practical and appropriate way.

Whilst this school is used as a case study model, the school itself was very humble in recognizing its own achievements and felt it was operating in a void somewhat, not knowing exactly what direction to take. While it is not my place to comment on the sound practice I was seeing, it was a point which emphasizes how schools should pool ideas and resources, using ideas as stimuli in much the same way as this text hopes to, particularly in a climate so keen to set school against school and effectively limit creativity in practice and thought. It is the role of teachers to make their own this vital foothold for the humanistic side of curriculum development amidst the rationality of centrally derived units of subject knowledge.

Chapter 5

VIEWS AND VISIONS

This chapter begins with a fairy tale, with thanks to Claire Tunney.

Once upon a time, the wise men of the land decided that the educationalists were not doing a good enough job, so they decreed that all the things which educationalists had been teaching anyway *must* now be taught. In order to make sure that these things were taught, they *wrote them down*. Many were the meetings and long were the consultations before the wise men decided that not only must the things be written down, they must also be written down *in order*. In this way, the educationalists would have no excuse for not doing a good job.

All agreed that some things were *very important* and so they wrote these down first. Next they wrote down those things which were only *important*. In order to ensure the very highest educational standards they also wrote down exactly how long it would take to teach each of those things correctly. However, here the men, both eminent and wide, hit a problem. They found that each thing they had written down was of such importance that an amazing 90 per cent of the time in school had been used up. This left only 10 per cent of the time for those other things that they really would like taught. Well, time was not permitting and not wishing to risk a lowering of standards in the 'very important' and the 'important' things they decided that they would write down all those other things as well, but call them the 'things education might embrace slightly'. Now they all were generally pleased with themselves but slightly troubled with the sound of 'Things education might embrace slightly' so to make the troubled feelings go away they shortened this statement to *themes*. All agreed that this sounded very good indeed, and the children of the nation learned happily ever after.

At this time, in the country, a headmaster decided that his school building was not quite good enough. Fortunately, being a man of foresight he had released his school from the clutches of Loony, his local education authority. This had meant that he had received pots of money from the wise men's coffers. The headmaster had a vision. He would use this pot of gold to build a fine school building that met the specifications proclaimed by the wise men – a more appropriate and less restrictive environment for pupils.

Like all sensible constructionists, he started with the foundations. To make his foundations the strongest and the best, he selected the best and strongest materials. On top of the foundations he laid the best bricks. Not all of the bricks fitted together perfectly, but they were such good bricks that this did not really matter. The headmaster was rigorous in his selection. He declared it 'important', nay 'very important' that any materials judged by him not to be up to standard were discarded immediately. The headmaster laboured long and hard to build his school. He was delighted to see that the new school buildings looked far better than those that had gone before. Truly, he wondered to himself, it was amazing that they had managed for so long without them.

Many came from all areas of the country to admire the new buildings. The people clamoured to see the newly completed work. All agreed that these were indeed far better than any other buildings they had seen. They were more compact and far more structurally sound. Indeed, the structure was envied by many. But gradually the admiration and envy evaporated. The crowd began to look closer and some started to express doubts about the quality of the building. It was even mentioned that there seemed to be no cohesion between the bricks themselves. The headmaster was horrified. The crowd looked closer still and gradually the problem became clear. In his haste to complete the buildings in time for the forthcoming academic year, the headmaster had neglected to apply cement. Well, time was really short now and the headmaster was forced to turn to the materials which had originally been discarded. As he surveyed the materials with a new zeal he was delighted to see that some of it was actually of very high quality. And so he ground these materials down and mixed them together to form a cement with which he was really quite pleased. The crowd renewed its clamouring and once again agreed that these were very fine buildings indeed. Parents jostled to send their children to the new improved school and the headmaster's future seemed bright. Opening day arrived and the headmaster began his celebratory speech. All were so dazzled by the impressiveness of the buildings and the fervour of the headmaster's words that nobody noticed the cracks beginning to appear in he walls . . .

Chapters 3 and 4 have shown ways in which the 'cement' holds the 'bricks' together to add quality to and enrich the learning opportunities of children within primary and secondary schools. These chapters reported examples that clearly demonstrated the implementation of challenging curriculum practices. Such practices were the result of careful planning, considered and thoughtful resource management, flexible and creative teaching and learning strategies and a high level of interactive involvement between teachers and students. This chapter focuses on the thoughts and feelings of the people who have a view about the nature of the 'cement' in the building – the structure of the National Curriculum and the place of cross-curricular work. Parent, pupil and teacher perspectives are considered in response to the questions:

- What is to be gained from engaging in cross-curricular work?
- How do they add to the statutory National Curriculum?
- What do they offer the pupils in the act of acquiring knowledge?

This chapter offers a platform for the voices of these different participants.

The pupils' voice

What do young people want from their education? How do they perceive it? In discussion with a group of 14-year-old students about to begin on their two-year course leading up to the GCSE (Key Stage 4), they highlighted aspects of their education that was important to them. The knowledge, skills and attitudes espoused through the cross-curricular themes emerged through the discussion as central to their perceived needs in preparing them for life beyond school. When asked about careers these were their comments.

We don't seem to study life outside school very much. It is all very well doing the subjects but we don't really see how they fit in. I mean, if you want to be a teacher you obviously think about some of the subjects you want to take, but we are not told how this will help you, or how it will fit into a job when you go and look at what you want to do for a living. We don't do much about handling people, talking to people and how to get on with people that perhaps you don't like.

Next year we have work experience and careers education. Rather than just waiting for our work experience we ought to explore the world of work in other years. We do work experience – that is a brilliant idea. Learning about careers is important. You might have a brilliant idea about doing something but you get in there and find you don't like it. It would be good if we had a chance to do more than just one week experience. In the third year (Year 9) is a good time because you choose your options at the end of the year, so you need to do it before we make our choices. I'd like a build up before the options. We could take an area of jobs and find out about it. It would be good if the teacher helped us then.

Pupils are generally keen to learn about their environment.

I think we should care about the world we live in. The environment will affect our children. We should cover what is happening at the moment. What is it like – is it bad and what can we do to help it. Everyone should learn to care for their environment; it should be brought into lessons. It might make people take more notice of what is being said. The environment is important, especially what would happen and how it might affect our children. We don't really know what we can do to help the environment. You get a lot of information from the TV. When we go to express our point of view, especially to adults, they say you don't know what you are talking about, so if we had lessons we would know what we were talking about.

Economic and industrial understanding is also seen as necessary.

We are not really being taught about the outside world and being prepared so they should do things about money and banks. That would help us. I don't have a clue how the economy works. It might be a good idea if we did something about that, and about controlling my own money. I have a bank account but don't know how it works or about interest or anything like that.

There is a need for information on citizenship.

We should be taught about our rights and responsibilities. Know things now so we are better prepared for the world after school. I'd like to learn more about what is going on in the world now. I'd like to learn about other countries of the world like South Africa and what it would be like under apartheid. We could do with a lesson to look at what is on the news and then talk about it. I don't understand about Maastricht for example. They should explain about that more. An opportunity to talk about the issues in the world to-day.

Even health care, traditionally thought covered, lacks relevance in some pupils eyes.

It wouldn't be a bad idea to learn about animal care. We get quite a bit about health, the nurse talks to us. Learning about contraception is a bit more important than learning about what is the highest mountain in the world!

Another group of pupils now in secondary school looked back on their project at Ipplepen school (the African Project described in Chapter 3). Amy Sanders, Jemma Ferguson, Suzie Clyne and Jeremy Ballie were very clear about the impact the project had on their personal and social development. Their words encapsulate the value of the explicit interrelation of PSE with subject knowledge. In the interview they began by describing the trip to London and their feelings about the the final product. They had performed the dance drama at the Barclay's Award in London.

When they announced that we had won the best chosen topic, I thought we had won the whole thing. We were really excited and I was jumping up and down and we won the best choreographic performance. We won them because we had tackled a hard subject. We got it for originality. We were really different from the others. We came second. The winners were from a Welsh drama school. Their acting was very good so we didn't mind coming second. It was a fun experience. We all enjoyed it because we saw each other all over again because we had left the school.

We first started doing the topic when Mr Parkins said, 'Right, we are going to do Africa.' Everyone said, 'Oh' and we were not really that interested. We were chatting and laughing; it meant nothing to us really. Then we heard about the apartheid system when Mr Parkins talked about it and we saw various newspaper cuttings. I think the majority of our class became very interested and we all got so involved, even spellbound at times because we were upset when we saw the way the black people were treated.

The things he said made us want to say things. People were standing up and making speeches and Mr Parkins was sitting there – I think he was surprised (but I think he was pleased as well) that we took to it so seriously.

When we finished our lessons and we were out in the playground, the whole playtime was devoted to talking about the apartheid system and the blacks and the whites and what we thought was fair and what we didn't.

At one point during the project Mr Parkins split the class – 75 per cent were black and 25 per cent white – and we had to be black or white for the day. The toilet had stickers and you had to go to certain toilets. The white people all got orange juice and biscuits in the middle of the lesson and we wanted some, saying please, but we didn't get any. It taught us a lesson. At the beginning of the day we felt as if we were normal because we were all friends and everything but when it came to this, we couldn't talk to each other or sit with each other. Blacks were made to sit in a different place. You really did feel left out because your friends, who were the whites, were all sitting and chatting and drinking this orange juice and eating these nice chocolate biscuits and you sat there thinking they are not paying any attention to me. I thought. 'They are my friends why don't they give me a bit of their chocolate biscuit and a taste of their orange juice' but they didn't. It didn't feel nice at all. That experience helped us a lot to understand.

We started off with a topic on Africa in the classroom and we wrote poems about the apartheid system but then it carried on from there. Our teacher is really into dance and drama. We did a lot of dance and drama anyway and Africa became the topic of the drama and the dance. Then we wrote some more poems and then it was turned into a production. The teacher basically sorted out where different parts went but we did it. We suggested ideas. All the dances were made up by us with the teacher.

Doing the topic made me want to go to Africa and find out more and understand more. If I hadn't done the topic I wouldn't have known about these things. It was not like a normal project. I learnt something new everyday about it. Things happened in the news and around you and it made me think, 'Why are they acting like that?' It made me think about the feelings of the people in that country. So that motivated us to start really caring about our dance and it just basically moved on from there.

I liked the part when we were the animals as well, the zebras and lions. I learnt about the way they moved. To move as an animal we had to study them and in our masks we tried to make the audience believe we were these animals.

Our school performances were about two hours and had lots more songs and dances in it than the version we took to London. We felt proud of ourselves and we did it about three or four times. Knowing we might perform it in London made us work harder on it.

When Mr Parkins asked who would like to do some speaking parts I said, 'OK, I would.' I had a small speech to say because I was a black and at the beginning I took it as a joke and I wasn't really trying it at all. I was messing about with it really, but when Mr Parkins started to read all about the Blacks and we got to know more, gradually I got to care about my part and what I was saying a lot more. I started to put much more feeling into it because I understood it. It was not just acting and just pretending to be angry. I could feel the anger that these people must feel. I said in the play:

It is all very well for him standing there
He can listen and look but what does he care.
We're poor, we're hungry we are all skin and bone.
He's rich and well fed and he can go home.

I said that but I yelled it, and I was pointing. I really took it out on the people that were sitting there. I was saying, 'Why should you have all the nice things? Why should you be sitting in this

103

theatre now watching all these nice little children do this nice little play and not thinking about anything bad or anyone else's troubles.' It taught me that I can stand up for people and I can say what I think. It is not always up to other people to say what I think for me.

After we had done it and just looking at all the problems they must have had, the situations the blacks have to face. Now when I find that I get uptight and upset about stupid things I think about it more . . . you realize that people have to cope with famine and drought while I get upset about losing a rubber! If I do get upset about petty things I say to myself, 'Stop it.'

The project, the play, the dancing, the singing, the performing – it made me think that I want to do something about prejudice. We can all talk but it is the getting up and doing something about it that matters.

The whole project was exciting, interesting and you felt that if you walked away and turned your back on the production, everything else would collapse. They actually needed you and even if you were only standing in the corner and singing a song and just being one of the scene setters you felt really, really, important and needed. That was just nice, that feeling of being important.

And, finally in answer to the question, 'Have you ever felt that before or since to the same extent?' – 'No, not in the same way' was the unanimous response.

Through all the classroom work and the way knowledge was treated in the classroom, these pupils were able to come to terms with new ideas and to express them in their drama. They were learning many things. Learning about themselves and each other, learning about a foreign country, mixing history, geography and English knowledge and skills – all permeated with the equal opportunities dimension. The final performance was a sense of completion of a project that had enabled them both to integrate knowledge and to be creative. They had each found their own voice to communicate what they felt and what they thought.

The teacher's voice

Communication across subjects is the key in the secondary school to encourage pupils to use their knowledge and skills in the very different learning contexts with which they have to cope. In the complex technological society in which they are growing up, the computer is an important tool with which they will communicate more and more. As well as being a powerful aid to learning in school and in further and higher education, the computer is now established as part of the work context in industry, commerce and the public and private service sector. Any young person who is not computer-literate will be seriously disadvantaged in the world of work. The National Curriculum introduced computer literacy in the form of information technology (IT) as part of the technology subject area with its own attainment target. An IT advisory teacher voices his concerns about seeing the responsibility of developing these skills as only within the domain of one subject area.

We, as an IT team, are all very much children first and we feel that if you give that up you give it all up. I think that is particular to a cross-curricular approach. The whole learning environment is about the teacher-child relationship.

IT should be perceived as a cross-curricular activity. Teachers do perceive it as such but many are not confident in the skills to put it into practice. The majority of it will be assessed by teachers and will rely on teacher judgement and integrity. Evidence will be collected across the IT strands in the form of an IT folder for each pupil.

I would like to think that cross-curricular work has a future in the secondary school. It is going to depend a lot on the culture of the school and very much on ways to make people see its context most of the time. You have to make the students go through the hoops or whatever, but you can 'piggy back', by which I mean, for example, what we have been doing recently in IT and EIU and careers education with English. Look at the programme of study for English. They have to write in a particular way. They can be using the IT because it is there as a resource and you can then state the actual context, which gives you the EIU label to it within that particular subject. You can make teachers see that they are doing it already. I think at the moment I am trying to cut away from the attitude – here is another bit to bolt on – and to say, 'You are doing it'. I am trying to raise people's eyes above the trench as it were to look at the bigger picture. Just doing it like that, you are going to be covering with one single piece of work a number of ATs. Also by doing that you are not going to compartmentalize knowledge so much. The students are going to see, and this is what post–16 is asking for, for students to have an appreciation of how the process flows from one area to another. If you take one of these cross-curricular themes it can flow from one subject area to another and by using IT as the recording process you can then have some sense of where it is going. But it does need planning. By doing that you can reduce teachers' anxieties and then they can see a place for the cross-curricular work.

The parent's voice

The Education Reform Act 1988 had as a central tenet the importance of giving parents a choice of education for their children. Choice is only choice when the opportunities are there to exercise that choice. This may be more possible when the parents can opt to send their children to one of a number of schools within a reasonable geographical area. However, the situation is very different for parents living in a rural environment with access (including free travel) to only one village primary school to which all the local children go. For parents who perceive sending their children to a school away from the community as socially isolationist, that choice is more an illusion than a reality. There are certain expectations that parents have about their children's school. The parent interviewed here is clear about what he feels to be important and is critical of the way that the school has had to organize its curriculum to meet the specifications laid down by the National Curriculum.

As a parent, those things that we would describe as cross-curriculum themes is rather limited since the way that the school presents its curriculum, in so far as it does at all to parents, is couched in terms of the ten National Curriculum subjects. Last week, we had the annual parent-teacher interview. The discussion was based on the primary subjects – the maths, English and science – but also on general social development and it seemed to me that the latter was as important in the view of the teachers as the subjects, and I value that. When it comes to cross-curricular themes and dimensions as we understand it, the only thing that has become visible to me is the integration of special needs children. That was a deliberate move by the school to accommodate a severely handicapped youngster in one of my daughter's classes. I think the school has managed that well. I think the children have adapted very well and speak positively about the child concerned. It is refreshing for me to hear the children speak of her as a complete human being rather than an oddity. Beyond that I have only been aware of the impression the National Curriculum has made. If anything one would describe the approach maintained by my daughters' teachers as traditional and, as it happens, I think my two children have flourished under that. They get a lot of compensation at home, so I am not unduly anxious about that, but I am anxious, and could become increasingly so, that their activities in school, because of the National Curriculum emphasis, become severely constrained. The teacher of my elder daughter, when we went to our annual meeting, was concerned to talk about her social development, which has been significant. She was a very retiring child and would always stand on the edge of things – she was not used to the rough and tumble of life. We have noticed a significant step forward and it is quite clear to me the teacher has been able to put that very much at the centre of my daughter's personal curriculum, and that is important. However, it seems to me that it has been squeezed in, or bolted on, rather than being integrated within the National Curriculum.

The examples of primary practice in Chapter 3 provided an insight into the way that creative, inventive and challenging teachers can offer children many opportunities to express themselves and to learn about the world around them through active participation. The richness of this in helping children to develop personally and socially is valued by parents. This parent is aware that these things are possible but not, unfortunately, in his children's school.

I am not conscious of other activities that have gone on outside the National Curriculum subjects in an integrated way. They do have a Christmas play but it is scripted by an outsider, the music is written and arranged by an outsider and the whole thing is imposed upon the children. The older ones get the key parts and the younger ones end up decorating the front of the stage. In June, they have an activity week for the older children and they always go to do windsurfing and the younger children have a day at the Butterfly Farm. So, there isn't much sign of adventurous work there. Also the local community has a lot to offer. It is a village school but school links with the village are very limited. For instance, one of the things they were asked to do was to draw an old building – there are lots of them in the village – but they were not asked to find out anything about the building they drew. They haven't engaged people in the community apart from the vicar. It is a church school and the religion is presented as a matter of fact. It is not presented as a belief or a faith and no other religious faiths are presented to the children or discussed. It is as if the Church of England Christianity is the way the world is. That is the impression I get. There was a child who spent a term at the school a year ago who was from Indonesia and she was in my elder daughter's class. For me, it was a wonderful opportunity for that class to explore another world, another culture, another faith and everything and as far as I know that opportunity wasn't taken at all. In fact it was my daughter herself who came back and said, 'Where is Indonesia?'. She wanted to find out and we got the books and various things and she explored it at home.

There are many ways to teach across the continuum – from the teacher as provider of the knowledge, using a teacher-directed style, to teacher as facilitator, involving the pupils in an active partnership by centring the work towards the pupils' interests and building on the knowledge they have already. Teachers engaged in cross-curricular work use a variety of teaching strategies, conscious that learners do not all learn in the same way. This parent, with two daughters, sees different approaches in their teachers' reporting.

Taking opportunities to explore or link across in a cross-curriculum way seems to be happening in the reception class but somehow is not present in the Key Stage 1 class. It seems to me that the style of the different reports from the two teachers concerned is evidence of this. There are key differences. In the Key Stage 1 case, it was very much an account of the curriculum with reference to my child; I think the National Curriculum encourages a certain kind of approach – the fragmentation of knowledge into a unitary structure and so it is those units that provide the basis for reporting. In the reception teacher's case, however, it was an account of my daughter with reference to the learning opportunities. In the reception class you have a young person with these things interlaced – the person, the inquisitiveness, the anxiety, the mathematical skills, the literacy skills – all part and parcel of that person. So the comments were very much more so about the person and how she was developing and using these subjects and other things as landmarks.

I see a close connection between the integration of subject knowledge across any boundaries, which is of course what cross-curricular themes are directed at, on the one hand and child-centred practices on the other. Now child-centred practices are less visible in my children's school than in many other schools but they are least visible in my elder daughter's class and the language the teacher uses and examples of work that my daughter does are all illustrations of this. In the reception class there is more evidence of child-centredness, which I suppose is to be expected in a reception class where exploratory activities are encouraged, and the child will naturally steer herself across boundaries in her natural exploration. I would like the school experience as my children go through school to be a very broad-based body of knowledge. I would like to see the subject boundaries minimized. I would not like my daughters to see curriculum in terms of units of study called mathematics, English and all the rest of it. I would much prefer them to see it as a whole body of knowledge. I believe in that way they would integrate their other experiences, their out-of-school experiences and their school knowledge more fully than is the case at present. What is visible to me at the moment is that some behaviours and some knowledge and some descriptions are seen as appropriate in the school context and others in the home context. Now, I would like to see the two part and parcel of one another. I would like to see a less tightly framed curriculum. I would like to see something that encouraged my children in having faith in their own abilities in exploratory work so that they could learn to become learners rather than learning to become receptacles.

Clearly the perspectives of the pupils, the teacher, and the parent in this chapter highlight a particular view of the usefulness, relevance and worthwhileness of cross-curricular work. The government attitude towards cross-curricular work for 5 to 16-year-olds over the last few years has been far from encouraging. A student teacher, Elizabeth Bradshaw, picked up this point in a postscript to an essay she wrote about cross-curricular themes at the end of 1992.

> In a recent issue of *Update*, the regular newsletter from the Association of Teachers and Lecturers (ATL), it was reported that ATL representatives had been told by NCC officials that the themes were no longer 'flavour of the month' with the council members. 'Apparently subjects are in and cross-curricular themes are most definitely out.' I believe that it would be a great loss to the curriculum if the themes were dropped. The themes, especially citizenship, appear to me to make up the 'moral heart' of the curriculum, promoting equal opportunities and a good sense of what is right. They also promote collaboration, working for the common good and creativity. The cross-curricular work helps to provide a balanced and broadly based curriculum and plays a vital role in the personal and social development of the students. I believe that all of this is necessary if we are to improve the society in which we live.

There is, however, a postscript to that postscript. In the interim report of July 1993 on the review of the National Curriculum commissioned by the Secretary of State for Education and chaired by Sir Ron Dearing, it is stated that there should be increased flexibility of content, teaching, learning and assessing within the National Curriculum structure. This frees up more time for teacher-initiated work and therefore greater opportunities and possibilities for cross-curricular work. The challenge will be for teachers to develop and implement a fully worked-through, permeation model of themes, dimensions and skills within the subject knowledge culture. An issue to address is how to assess and evaluate the quality of such work. This is the subject of Chapter 6.

Chapter 6

EVALUATION AND ASSESSMENT OF CROSS-CURRICULAR WORK IN SCHOOLS

The opening chapter of this book set the agenda for cross-curricular work, by discussing the whole curriculum of the school. The point was made that schools are expected to educate children so that they can participate successfully in our society. The philosophy behind the school curriculum was described as the provision of a broad, balanced and differentiated curriculum aiming to give equal access to all children to achieve and to realize their potential. This book so far has sought to show how the cross-curricular themes, skills and dimensions can bring this philosophy to life: the emphasis on integrating propositional knowledge with practical and productive knowledge; relating life in the classroom with everyday life in the community; and developing personal and social knowledge in young people. Schools acquire information about whether the cross-curricular programmes they offer are indeed helping towards achieving these aims through the process of evaluation, and we acquire information as parents, teachers and employers about the achievements of individual children through the assessment process. This chapter is in two sections: the first explores and discusses an approach to evaluating cross-curricular work designed to help schools improve their practice; and the second suggests the style of assessment that will highlight the learning pupils have achieved through participating in such programmes.

Evaluating cross-curricular work in schools

Local management of schools (LMS) means that schools are given the majority of their budget directly. They have control over that money and therefore have to manage how they spend that money themselves. Increased control over the spending of their funds – on maintenance of the buildings, the non-teaching and teaching staff salaries, the heating, lighting, resources and curriculum – has brought with it not only a greater financial responsibility but also a greater accountability to the government and the community they serve; they are now required to provide detailed information about their educational intentions, practices and achievements. As well as on-going local accountability in the form of an annual report to parents, each school can now expect a general inspection at least once every four years. The myriad of administrative paperwork that arises out of the necessity to provide this information to justify school curriculum plans can be so overwhelming that school managers could find themselves setting up accountability systems that fulfil the purpose of giving information to outside interested parties but fail to be of value to the teachers in the school. The challenge is therefore to devise an accountability strategy that satisfies the needs of both the external and the internal communities, i.e. the accountability system should be so structured that it includes systematic collection of information as evidence to aid decision-making in the areas of curriculum review. The teachers' central concern is to improve the quality of learning in classrooms. They are becoming increasingly aware that the tangible evidence, provided by such a rigorous and systematic data-collecting exercise, opens up the possibilities for informed discussions with colleagues, based on more than the professional expertise and judgements they continue to make as part of their everyday work. This increases mutual understanding about the different curriculum activities in which they are engaged and helps them, in a collaborative way, to judge the worth of what they are doing. Another name for judging the worth of some thing is evaluation.

Development and change in teaching and learning can be viewed as teachers changing their curriculum practices – introducing new materials and new technology to support, facilitate and complement the teaching strategies they employ

– and as teachers changing their approach to the curriculum and the whole concept of learning in order to implement the changes in the classroom. The teachers find themselves also as learners, and evaluation plays a key role in this. As one secondary school curriculum co-ordinator states:

> If we as teachers do not take control of our own environment, we shall find ourselves at the mercy of others. We have to develop the skills of understanding the educational processes we are part of and be able to articulate them to others and we need to have the evidence that the kind of work we are doing has value, worth and merit. Evaluation is a way of doing that. It helps us to understand by forcing us to reflect in practice and we can only reflect as a community of teachers if we have collected information that we can use to not only help us plan and manage the changes but to provide the means to justify and articulate what we are about, to others.

This style of evaluation is underpinned by an educational research approach known as action research. Nixon (1981) writes that action research is about teachers investigating and reflecting on their own practice. Action research is practical research that asks for teachers to be researchers, to decide on the problems to be investigated and to use their own research findings to improve their practice as a result of reflecting and deliberating on present practice. Certain research skills are employed: listening, observing, recording and interviewing. Teachers possess these skills, using them every day in their work in classrooms. Action research simply utilizes them in a less familiar way.

The curriculum evaluation that focuses on school activities as advocated in this chapter employs action research principles and procedures, but is framed within a more specifically focused investigation. Eraut *et al.* (1987, p. 12) provide a suitable definition:

> Evaluation is (a) the collection, analysis, interpretation and reporting of evidence, (b) about the nature, impact and the value of the entity being evaluated, (c) with due attention to concerns and issues identified by the various interested parties.

This definition clearly states that something specific has to be identified at the outset (the entity) as the subject of the evaluation. In other words, the collection of the data has an explicit purpose, known to all interested parties. That purpose is not only to evaluate the entity itself – which could be a cross-curricular course, a particular approach to cross-curricular practices e.g. the use of information technology across the curriculum, or teaching and learning styles – but also the impact of the entity on the participants, as well as the intrinsic and extrinsic value of the entity. Key notions inherent in this definition are specific targeting, making informed judgements based on evidence, collecting perceptions of individuals involved and reporting on completion of the evaluation. Evaluation is an open, manageable activity that is essentially school-based and practical.

A school-based procedural model for evaluating cross-curricular work

School-based evaluation strives to support decision-making in schools. Eraut *et al*. (1987) list the following ways.

- providing evidence;
- presenting arguments;
- clarifying issues;
- suggesting ways of thinking; and
- making recommendations

School-based evaluation asks searching questions about the nature of school practices, which makes it highly appropriate for evaluating cross-curricular elements – a problematic area for schools. Fundamentally, it means that the school develops a 'critical' perspective – critical in the sense that it is not afraid to challenge underlying assumptions about practice and to ask, of itself, challenging questions. This is a highly sensitive area because it can make people feel uncomfortable, but questioning and developing go hand in hand. This approach to evaluation links the professional development of teachers with curriculum development for children: a model of how to proceed in carrying out an evaluation that helps both professional and curriculum development is offered here. There are three stages in the procedural model:

1. setting up the evaluation brief;
2. carrying out the evaluation process; and
3. disseminating the evaluation findings.

Setting up the evaluation brief
It is important before any evaluation activity starts – that the head of the school and the deputy head or senior manager whose job specification includes the implementation of cross-curricular work endorses the evaluation activity. In order for the exercise to be of any value to the school it must have the support of senior management, who will then be expected to consider the evaluation findings in order to inform school policy. Also, since the evaluation will have resource and time implications for the teacher carrying out the activity, this aspect will need to be negotiated with senior management beforehand. Once the evaluation is approved, the brief is worked out by the evaluator assigned the task, in association with a group of interested personnel in the school. In a small primary school this may involve the whole staff; in a secondary school it may be the team responsible for the teaching of the particular cross-curricular theme that is to be the subject of the evaluation, or it might be, for example, a faculty team if the issue is whether IT is being adequately addressed in Year 9 or not. The evaluator may or may not be the cross-curricular co-ordinator but whoever does take on the task for this specific evaluation activity will have senior management support.

The brief is specific, manageable, coming within the resources of the school, and is in three parts:

1. purpose – a statement of the focus of the evaluation;
2. means – specifying exactly as to how the information is to be collected; and

3. timescale – a target is set regarding the time by which the data is to be collected and when the final report is to be ready.

The following serves as an example of an evaluation brief.

Purpose

This will be an evaluation of the humanities faculty contribution to the Year 9 IT cross-curricular programme. It will focus on the quality of the IT experience by investigating the impact that the short modules of cross-curricular work being integrated into the humanities teaching programmes are having on both pupils and teachers. This is a matter of growing concern as discussions are now in progress about ways of implementing the cross-curricular themes, and short modules are being seen as a possible way for faculties to introduce easily identifiable cross-curricular elements in their courses.

Means

Information will be collected from a number of sources and in a number of ways. The six humanities teachers involved will be asked to complete a questionnaire distributed after the completion of the first module of IT work. Following an initial analysis of the questionnaire responses, three of the six teachers will be interviewed to discuss in greater detail the issues raised by the questionnaire. These interviews will be taped so that the interviewees will be able to comment on their own interviews.

Students of one Year 9 class (26 students) will complete questionnaires both before and after the modules of IT work. Four of these students will be followed up with a group taped interview, to develop some of the issues raised in the questionnaires. The students will be able to comment on the tape of the interview.

Timescale

Teacher questionnaire – end of Easter term
Teacher interviews – week 8 in summer term

Student questionnaires – through summer term
Student group interview – week 9 summer term

Report ready – week 12 summer term

The evaluation process

The evaluation process involves both formative and summative evaluation. Formative evaluation is defined as an investigatory and disciplined enquiry that provides information that increases understanding. Summative evaluation gives the overall effects, reporting on the relative strengths and weaknesses of the entity, highlighting issues to be addressed and/or making recommendations. The fact that it is school-focused, and initiated and conducted by teachers, promotes the formative aspect of the evaluation as part of the process. This is recognized in three ways:

1. Communicative – sets up discussion in the school and provides a means of communication on focused issues;
2. Participatory – gives individual teachers the opportunity to articulate their concerns to the evaluator; and
3. Knowledge base – broadens the information base and understanding of the people in the school by the sharing of different perspectives and perceptions.

The evaluation brief is now turned into an action plan. This stage includes the drawing up of the data-collecting instruments, e.g. the structuring of questionnaires. The operation of the timescale would also be worked out. Actual dates would be agreed upon between the evaluator and the contributors regarding the completion of questionnaires and the date, time, place and length of any interviews. Also, the time planned for the analysis of the interviews and the writing of the report needs to be worked out. Once the data have been collected, the evaluation activities of analysing and reporting are carried out. For example this may have two phases: the first would take place after any questionnaires were completed and verbal reporting to some of the evaluation contributors would take place at the time of the interviews; and the second phase would be the interview analysis and the writing up of the final summative report. In the example given above, the report might document the issues that the evaluation found needed to be addressed under the headings of those relating to faculty planning, access to IT equipment, quality of learning material, etc. and an assessment of achievement made as to the value of using such modules as a cross-curricular implementation model.

Dissemination

As the school community has control over the information collected, it has ownership of the evaluation report. It is its responsibility to make use of and to find value in the evaluation process undergone in the previous stage. Reports should be short, precise and easy to read. Issues and practices are identified, not individuals. If the evidence has been collected in a systematic way then all the information is available as evidence but it need not all be included in the summative report. The report should deal succinctly with findings, beginning with the statement of evaluation brief and then listing the various issues and/or the recommendations, followed by sufficient evidence to show how and why these judgements have been reached.

In summary therefore this model of evaluation is a tool to aid professional development. Teachers who have engaged in this style of evaluation claim that they see an association between their own development as teachers and the impact their practice has on pupils. Specifically they state that they see it as having provided a way of:

- approaching evaluation that is formative and developmental but at the same time coming up with a product that gives them information on which to act;
- looking at the work that is going on in the school that encourages reflection on practice that is 'critical' but not destructive;
- encouraging teachers to listen to one another and to listen to pupils;
- providing teachers with information that is based on evidence as opposed to 'hearsay', rumour and anecdotes;

- involving teachers in understanding and illuminating working practices across the curriculum; and
- giving teachers the opportunity to feel a sense of ownership in improving their own professional practice.

Assessing pupils' achievements

Traditionally assessment, certainly in the minds of education policy-makers, has been synonymous with examinations – conceived as a competitive device and designed to select out the more academically able from the less able. As Roach (1971, p. 3) succinctly puts it:

> Public examinations were the great discovery of the nineteenth century Englishman. Almost unknown at the beginning of the century, they rapidly became a major tool of social policy.

This situation has not changed. Indeed, in 1985, a Government White Paper, *Better Schools* (DES 1985, p. 29), endorsed this aspect of the value of examinations.

> For most people the period of compulsory education culminates in assessment through public examination. The Government believes this should continue to be so. Examination results are one important means of assessing achievement; examinations properly designed are a stimulus to good performance and parents and employers, as well as pupils, rightly value them.

The culmination of compulsory schooling in assessment terms, is the 16+ examination system (the General Certificate of Secondary Education) which operates as an accountability factor for the government; the pupils' gradings in the GCSE examinations determine the kind of education and/or training they will then have access to especially when there is competition for finite resources. In each of the main subjects there are nationally prescribed criteria i.e., even though pupils might sit an examination in, say, mathematics set by an examination board in the north of England, it will examine very similar concepts and understandings to an examination set by a board in the south of England because rules and guidelines laid down by the government will operate in both

cases. The existence of common criteria within the GCSE has
given the politicians a basis for establishing the idea that
schools' educational achievements could be reasonably judged
by comparing the GCSE results of one school with another.
These two notions of selection and competition have been
transposed into the new arrangements for National Curriculum assessment. The GCSE has become the final assessment
point in a centrally imposed assessment scheme that has
external standardized assessments for all children at ages 7,
11 and 14 as well as 16.

Over the past seven years, since the introduction of the
GCSE, political emphasis in the educational arena has
increasingly concentrated on promoting this accountability
aspect of assessment. This is clearly demonstrated by the
developments in the debate between educationalists and politicians with regard to the design of the national assessments
at key ages: 7, 11 and 14 years old. In 1987, in preparation
for the 1988 Education Act coming into force, the Secretary
of State for Education invited a group of educationalists to
advise him and the national curriculum working groups 'on
the overriding requirements which should govern assessment
and testing in schools for children of all abilities at the key
ages of around 7, 11, 14 and 16' (DES press release, 30 July
1987). The Task Group on Assessment and Testing (TGAT),
chaired by Professor Paul Black, was given until Christmas
1987 to carry out this task. The story of TGAT (the initial
acceptance of the report and then the subsequent under-
mining of the key principles inherent in its structure) clearly
demonstrates real differences between educationalists and
politicians' views and understandings of the value and purpose of assessment and the effect that a national assessment
system would have on teaching, learning and educational
achievement. This section of the chapter first examines the
differences between the educationalist's view of assessment
and the politician's view, then goes on to discuss possible ways
in which achievements within cross-curricular work can be
recognized and incorporated into the national assessment
system.

Different views of assessment

The members of the group responsible for the TGAT report were assessment specialists with many years experience in the development of assessment techniques and of tests for public examinations. Some were also members of the government's Assessment and Performance Unit set up in the late 1970s to monitor national standards. They were aware of the impact that assessment had on teaching and learning. Black (1988) stated

> The Task Group could not be accused of evading its task by playing down the importance of assessment ... The implication is that the Group assumed that assessment information, produced through a system that provides uniform terms and criteria that command confidence, and also respects and works with the professional expertise and responsibility of teachers, would be a valuable asset.

This desire to mesh together the merits and functions of both classroom and external assessment led to the report proposing that teacher assessment and standard assessment tasks were to be complementary and to serve 'several purposes... formative... diagnostic... summative... evaluative' (TGAT 1988, para 23). It would be formative i.e. provide information on where the pupil is now, which would help teachers plan the next stages of learning, and diagnostic in that it would enable more detailed diagnostic scrutiny where special problems exist. It would be summative, which means providing overall evidence of achievements of individual pupils, and evaluative because the aggregation of information about numbers of pupils would make it possible to assess curriculum issues as well as flag problems of resources and so on.

The TGAT group came up with the following recommendations. Up to the age of 16 the assessments would be essentially formative with teacher assessments (TAs) playing a central role. The assessments would provide information for teachers to use in giving feedback to pupils and parents as well as helping to develop plans for progression to the next stage of learning. The function of the standard assessment tasks (SATs) – common assessment tasks administered and marked in the same way by all teachers – would be to provide comparability across schools of the same Key Stage pupils. These SATs would be close to classroom activities and employ a variety of modes of presentation. Summative and evaluative purposes would be served by aggregation of the formative assessments, both the TAs and the SATs, at the level of profile components in each of the subjects at the end of the key stages. This would provide information to governors, LEAS and the general public. Pupils would each have a Record of Achievement (RoA) to record progress and achievement within the system.

These recommendations from the report of the Task Group on Assessment and Testing were closely followed by the test constructors of the pilot SATs for Key Stage 1. These initial SATs generated problems for primary school teachers mainly because in there was no history of administering systematic formal assessment procedures for children at the age of 7. The teachers experienced the kind of problems one would expect when a new system is implemented without a reasonable time-scale of preparation; anxiety, administrative difficulties, and workload. These difficulties provided the opportunity for the Secretary of State for Education, Kenneth Clarke, under the powers granted him by the Education Reform Act 1988, to substantially reformulate and simplify the SATs. In the Westminster Lecture of June 1992 he clearly stated his principles of assessment in a highly political way.

> The British pedagogue's hostility to written examinations of any kind can be taken to ludicrous extremes. The British left believes pencil and paper examinations impose stress on pupils and demotivates them. We have tolerated for 20 years an arrangement whereby there is no national testing or examination of any kind for most pupils until they are 16 . . . This opposition to testing and examinations is largely based on a folk memory in the Left about the old debate of the 11+ and grammar schools.

The Secretary of State for Education limited the SATs at Key Stage 1 and stipulated that at Key Stage 3 there would be National Curriculum tests (NC tests). It has also been ruled that the NC tests are to be the only evidence reported on except in the case of practical and performance attainment targets which are not susceptible to pencil and paper tests. These would be assessed by teachers. These decisions have had the effect of reducing the breadth and variety of educational achievements assessed through standardized national assessment. Also by raising the status of the SATs at Key Stage 1 and the NC tests at Key Stage 3, teacher assessment has been downgraded. The first NC tests for Key Stage 3 were to take place in June 1993 and reported to the public in the form of National Curriculum levels of attainment but the massive opposition by teachers about the nature of these tests led to a boycott orchestrated by professional groups like NATE (National Association of English Teachers) and all the teacher unions. The teachers felt the tests to be flawed and the overriding principles of TGAT as having been abandoned. The point about the flawed nature of the tests had already been made by the chair of TGAT, Professor Paul Black, in his presidential address to the education section of the British Association for the Advancement of Science on 25 August 1992 (and reported in the *TES* on 28 August 1992).

> ... a return to tests of poor validity, dangerous unreliability, and a heritage of damaging effects on pupils' learning. It is not clear why these traditional tests are so preferred – it appears that they bear the image of 'traditional values' in this field, that they might have the advantage that teachers who are not to be trusted are not involved in them, perhaps even that they must be good because the 'pedagogues' and/or the 'left wing' don't like them ... Those who gave dire warnings that the Education Reform Act would be an instrument for direct government control in which the opinions of ministers would be insulated from professional opinion and expertise have been proved correct.

Formal assessment throughout the whole schooling system seems to driven by political imperative rather than educational reasoning. This political intrusion into educational practice is seen by Black to stress the political purposes of assessment, those of selection, grading and competition, and thus to weaken a fundamental principle of TGAT, the criterion-referencing assessment targets which would have made it possible for pupils to have been entered for SATs at the time they were ready during the progression from key stage to key stage. Instead, pupils were to sit NC tests at the same time – another name for a public examination – with the assessment sorting out the more from the least able, just as the GCSE examination does. So clearly the formative element built into TGAT has receded, moving the whole process of systematic assessment to a series of snapshot summative assessments of individual pupils, i.e. each child is perceived to be on a level in the subject, with the levels publicly reported for the evaluative function of comparing the school with school.

NC assessment has an effect on all levels of teaching and learning. Teachers have to record their assessments of pupils regularly and be able to justify the levels they record, if asked. School learning revolves around the direct linkage between the prescribed programmes of study of the school subjects and the attainment targets reported on. Assessment will be very detailed, describing the process of gathering, interpreting, recording and using information about pupils' responses to an educational task. School knowledge, packaged and delivered in the discrete subject units, is to be controlled from the age of 5 to 16 through this systematically administered mechanism of assessment.

This shift will make it difficult to integrate assessment with work that is interdisciplinary in nature, work that incorporates the cross-curricular themes into teaching programmes. These political directives are moving assessment practices in schools back to being predominantly objectively focused, concentrating on the outcomes of learning that can be quantitatively measured. This raises issues about the relationship of assessment to learning, to pupil motivation and to inclusion in the curriculum of learning experiences that are not easily assessable in quantifiable and measurable units. There is a real danger that this will reduce the time and resources for undertaking the more subjectively focused qualitative modes of assessing which have been purposefully and productively developing in schools during the last decade. There are genuine concerns about the negative effects low achievement or failure in tests and examinations have on pupils and the psychological effects that school failure is seen to have on the future life chances of pupils, especially if the child leaves the school system with a poor national assessment record of positive achievements.

Examinations have been part of schooling for a long time so these psychological arguments are not new. However, as already mentioned, over the last decade educationalists have attempted to address these concerns by redefining the parameters of assessment. Sally Brown (1990, p.5) discusses this new approach to assessment in the following way.

> Change can be unsettling sometimes overwhelming, but it can also be motivating and bring about real progress. In the field of assessment, a great deal of talk over the last decade has been about change and substantial attempts have been made to introduce new practices. Different practices usually reflect different ideological commitments, and one of the most salient features of the movement has been the recognition that assessment, as part of education, must be about promoting learning and opportunities, rather than sorting people into social roles for society.

Recognizing that assessment should promote learning and opportunities has stimulated the notion that educational assessment should provide a broader range of information about pupils' accomplishments. This has led to a much broader conceptualization of assessment. Assessment, from the educationalists' point of view, is no longer equated simply with testing and, through testing, selection. Assessment is seen to fulfil multiple purposes. The TGAT (1988) report is an example of the attempt to interrelate within a single system these multiple purposes. In such a system classroom and external assessment are meshed together, with formative and summative assessment seen as complimentary. The TGAT group's perceptions of the different approaches to assessing, i.e. the making of qualitative judgements by

teachers as a necessary counterbalance to quantifiable externally set objective tests is clearly expressed in the purposes
and principles section of the report. Paragraph 42 states:

> The term 'assessment' is used to refer to an individual component
> of the total assessment process or to a particular method of assess-
> ment. Hence, it encompasses all procedures used to make an esti-
> mate or appraisal of an individual's achievement. Which of the
> many methods of assessment may be appropriate in particular
> circumstances will depend on the purpose of the assessment.

Conceiving assessment more broadly makes it possible to consider assessing a far wider range of qualities. Certain qualities, e.g. critical thinking, self-knowledge, invention,
formulating new questions, making inferences, creativity,
empathy, and sensitivity to others, are not susceptible to being
assessed through highly structured, standardized pencil and
paper tests. Assessment strategies that focus on the product
of pupils' thinking rarely offer qualitative insights into the
thinking processes themselves. In recent years, assessment
strategies have been developed that offer insights into the
quality of pupils' learning processes in order to reveal achievements already gained and to improve on them (Tyler, 1986;
Wood, 1987; Frederikson and Collins, 1989; Paris *et al.*, 1991).

An interesting example of this is the findings of the American research into assessment in the arts funded by the Rocke-
feller Foundation in 1985, which was set up to develop
'powerful versions' of qualitative models of assessment (Wolf
1987/88).

> The lack of powerful qualitative information about student learn-
> ing, thoughtful ways of using that information, and training for
> educators in this kind of assessment is a major gap in the way
> American educators go about indexing and studying student
> learning.

This study found ways of tapping into the essential qualities
of education by focusing on assessment modes that made
visible the individual's ability to formulate novel problems,
engage in a number of thinking processes and reflect on the

quality of his or her own work. The 'making visible' was through teachers refining their assessment skills by 'reading' their students' 'biographies' of progress as demonstrated in their portfolios and engaging in reflective interviews which gave opportunity for teachers and students together to stand back and think about the work the students had produced.

It is generally recognized that traditional assessment techniques are more suited to assessing the transmission of propositional knowledge than to assessing individual understandings of social knowledge and personal qualities – qualities and understanding that permeate pupils' work and are a valued and important dimension of teaching and learning, the central concern of cross-curricular work. Qualitative assessment is concerned with the generation of information about the pupils' understandings and ways of knowing. It involves encouraging pupils to describe their processes of learning and teachers to talk to their pupils about their working practices and achievements. This type of assessment is about qualitative judgements, not quantitative measurement, and there exists one area of the national assessment system that can offer opportunities to incorporate these strategies: teacher assessment. Teacher assessment of the National Curriculum is on-going alongside the external set tests. It could be argued that this need not bind the teachers to a narrow conception that mirrors the externally constructed assessments. As the SEAC (1991) document on Teacher Assessment at Key Stage 3 states:

> Teacher assessment is an integral part of teaching and learning in the classroom. Teachers discuss with pupils, guide their work, ask and answer questions, observe, encourage, challenge, help and focus. In addition, they mark and review written work and other outcomes. Through these activities they are continually finding out about their pupils' capabilities and achievements. This knowledge then informs plans for future work. It is this continuous process that comprises teacher assessment.

The approach to assessment of cross-curricular work which is centrally concerned with personal qualities, social knowledge and practical productive work lies within the domain of pupil-teacher direct interaction, integrated with the teaching and learning process. The purpose of assessment as informing and improving learning is recognized and the teacher as professional is placed at the heart of the process.

Recording achievement

The alternative perspective on assessment described in this chapter is the appropriate strategy for assessing pupils' learning through cross-curricular work. It will give access to pupils' thinking and problem-solving and creative processes. It will enable the teacher and pupil to sit down together and discuss processes and outcomes. The evidence of qualitative assessment is meaningfully recorded through descriptive statements. Therefore, a key requirement for valuing qualitative assessment practices is the incorporation of descriptive statements into the educational assessment system alongside marks and grades, with the pupils receiving a summary document that describes actual achievements. This document is known as a record of achievement (RoA).

Torrance (1989), in reviewing assessment developments, generally articulates two important principles that underlie the RoA process which has been developing in schools since the introduction of TVEI:

1. the desire to assess and record achievements other than, or at least additional to, those which are subject based – personal development, the capacity to contribute to a group, to work independently, and so forth (p. 187);
2. the involvement of pupils in the process of interaction with their teachers in dialogue and negotiation about their statements of attainment. It was argued that this would heighten their awareness and encourage them to reflect on both the processes and outcomes of their learning. This involvement in their own assessment would help them to become more responsible for their own learning.

The major difference between the RoA movement and traditional assessment is the central focus of assessment. Within the RoA perspective, learners play an active and central role, mapping attainments and accomplishments with the help of their teacher. Within traditional assessment, the curriculum objectives are central, with learners placed on a grid of pre-specified attainments.

Broadfoot (1988), who directed the pilot Records of Achievement in Schools Evaluation (PRAISE), expresses clearly these two different approaches in her response to the national assessment system.

> Records of Achievement are premised on the assumption that better teaching, better relationships between teachers and pupils, clearer objectives, a sense of achievement and more relevant educational goals will combine to produce a more lively and rewarding educational experience for pupils. National Assessments on the other hand are premised on the assumption that goals should be the same for everyone, that they are still essentially subject-based, that they are pre-defined and systematically assessed and that motivation comes predominantly from competition rather than co-operation and a sense of achievement for the majority.

There is a place for both these forms of assessment in schools, the giving of marks and grades and the recording of achievement through descriptive statements. They can complement each other, thus giving a more fully rounded picture of the diversity of the child's achievements in school.

Endnote

This chapter has indicated that schools can evaluate cross-curricular activities in a way that helps to shape and form good practice, offering a range of challenging and interesting learning experiences for pupils that integrate different knowledge areas and enable young people to participate and thus to develop personal and social skills and understandings. The discussion on assessment clarifies the way it is possible, through these curriculum activities, for teachers and pupils to assess the quality of learning that has taken place. The pupils should be credited for what they have achieved through the formal recording of their achievements within their National RoA file.

Chapter 7

CONCLUSION: THE FUTURE FOR CROSS-CURRICULAR WORK?

It is worth remembering that the National Curriculum was introduced to promote the spiritual, moral, cultural, mental and physical development of pupils at school and of society through the establishment of a broad and balanced curriculum. It was realized and accepted that the ten National Curriculum subjects and Religious Education were not expected to manage this aim alone. They had to be augmented by additional subjects beyond the ten National Curriculum subjects: extra-curricular activities and an accepted range of cross-curricular elements in order for pupils to develop the knowledge, understanding and skills which they, and the country, will need in the twenty-first century. Such a laudable aim had general agreement from all sectors of the educational establishment, but the style and method of the implementation of the National Curriculum has met with criticism, dissatisfaction and, in many cases, outright opposition. The move from policy to practice, the managing of such a wholesale curriculum change, has been party to two fundamental flaws.

The first fundamental flaw was the way the then Secretary of State for Education, Kenneth Baker, set up the National Curriculum. He established ten separate working groups for each of the National Curriculum subjects to decide the content of the subject. As Wragg (1993) commented in the *Observer*: 'It is a recipe for disaster. Lock separate groups of subject enthusiasts away in ten different rooms for a few weeks and they all return wanting half the week for their own discipline.' And this is virtually what happened. The result of such a process was that each subject group defined the content of each Order, i.e. what knowledge is to be taught in each subject under the law. There was no overview, no collective judgement made about the effect that putting these subjects together would have on the teaching and learning of the curriculum as a whole. Also each Order was very prescriptive and content-laden. Fulfilling the terms of the Orders has meant that teachers have been very restricted, finding it increasingly difficult to be creative and flexible and to exercise professional judgements to meet the needs of their particular pupils.

As Director of the School of Education at the University of Exeter, Professor Wragg has been consistently raising this issue with the Government since the 1988 Education Act. Even well before the Act, he raised awareness about the problems that would emerge if the schooling system was driven by political imperatives as opposed to educational ones. In 1980 he wrote an article entitled, ten steps down the slippery slope to state-approved knowledge and by 1993 he makes the point that all ten steps had materialized.

> Now all ten are in place, as the Government controls the detail of what is taught, how it is tested and what happens to test scores, and even begins to attack teaching methods and prescribe the books children should read. (Wragg, 1993)

As each individual subject is prescriptive, constrictive and content-laden, this has caused implementation problems in the schools in terms of manageability. How do you manage to do all that is asked for in the time available? Hargreaves (1991 p. 36) points this out clearly.

> Greater breadth was a key purpose behind the National Curriculum reforms. As all teachers know, the broader the curriculum becomes, the greater the problem of manageability. The problem is easily stated: how to get the quart of a desirable curriculum into the pint pot of the school timetable. To ensure that pupils receive the broad curriculum to which they are entitled requires a solution to the problem that there seems to be insufficient room for it. The civil servants who drew up the consultation document (DES, 1987) on the National Curriculum ran into this problem, of course. Probably unwisely, they illustrated the curriculum in the last two years of compulsory schooling. Once they had listed

the core and foundation subjects and some reasonable time allocations for them, they had used up some 80–90% of curriculum time, if account is taken of RE. This left just 10–20% for a second modern language, classics home economics, business studies, careers education, PSE and a whole range of cross-curricular material.

Not only is it difficult to manage the aim of a broad and balanced curriculum but there is another problem: one of coherence at the level of content and also at the level of pupils experiencing coherence between the subjects and within and between the five cross-curricular themes and the subjects. As Hargreaves (1991, p. 37) further states: 'This is a massive task of curriculum co-ordination but it is on the quality of this co-ordination that both content and experiential coherence for the curriculum as a whole rests'. This book is witness to the fact that there have been creative and successful approaches to this problem of coherence by individual teachers and schools. Coming to grips with the issues of manageability and coherence with such odds stacked against them demonstrates the quality of professional practice in so many of our schools. However, under the National Curriculum and assessment arrangements that have been put in place up to this time of writing there is a limit to what the teachers, alone, can do.

This brings us to the second fundamental flaw in the implementation of the National Curriculum: the issue of the assessment arrangements. The development of the National Curriculum assessment system was discussed in Chapter 6, which indicated the concerns expressed by teachers and others about the pre-eminence of testing throughout the whole system, the relationship between those proposed tests and teacher assessment and the purposes to which the information from the summative tests would be put. It is also the case that teachers are expected to assess pupils continuously against the numerous statements of attainments with the subject Orders and show evidence of pupils' achievements through time-consuming and complex assessment recording devices. However, in the final analysis, it was to be the National Curriculum tests alone at Key Stage 3 that were to be published to denote the achievement levels of the pupils. Teacher assessment did not have equal parity. As the Key Stage 3 tests of June 1993 approached, the increased concerns of parents and governors about the testing programme gave an added impetus to the proposed boycott of the tests promoted by the teacher unions, which was overwhelmingly supported by teachers. Conscious that there was ardent and vocal denouncement of the tests, the Secretary of State for Education, John Patten, in April 1993, instigated a review of the current National Curriculum and Assessment framework hoping, perhaps, that the promise of a review might weaken the resistance to the testing programme. However, the boycott remained in place and, consequently, very little testing took place in June 1993 at Key Stage 3. The review went ahead under the direction of Sir Ron Dearing. He consulted widely with schoolteachers through written statements sent into his office and through a number of regional conferences set up for that purpose. The interim report of the Dearing Review, published in July 1993, shows evidence that he did listen to the very real concerns of teachers. The Government accepted Sir Ron Dearing's report, which included streamlining the assessment system. He recommended that in 1994 there should be only statutory national testing and assessments for the subjects of English, mathematics and science at each of the Key Stages 1, 2 and 3. Teacher assessment and test results are given equal status and there is recognition that the two have different purposes and therefore complement each other, and so they will be kept separate. The equality of weighting between external tests and teacher assessment should help to develop assessment practices that recognize the creative, personal and social achievements of young people and give added status to the notion of recording clear and jargon-free statements about individual accomplishments in the RoA as well as in school reports to parents. This can only augur well for cross-curricular work to be assessed and reported on if sufficient time is built into the curriculum organization of the school.

In this respect of manageability and developing coherence across the curriculum for pupils, the Dearing Review had something else to contribute. Sir Ron recommended that the National Curriculum should be streamlined, suggesting the following approach to revising the curriculum Orders (1993, Para 3.36, p. 34).

> During consultation much weight has been placed by teachers and many others on the need for a fully integrated approach to revisions of the curriculum resulting from the Review. The purpose of these revisions would be to slim down the content and the degree of prescription in the present Orders through the identification of the essential core of knowledge, understanding and skills in each subject. All schools would be required by law to teach this core. Remaining elements of the current Order would be retained as optional, enrichment material.

Such an approach will lead to fewer statutory and more non-statutory elements within the subject curriculum. This should make the subject curriculum more flexible, thus increasing the possibilities for across-subject and subject-and-theme integration to develop over the next few years.

Pupils themselves value such integration. Certainly the pupil group I talked to who were involved in the Africa Project were very aware of the different organizational structure within the secondary school that, in their six months' experience of it, was not offering them the same opportunities as the primary school for continuing with a cross-curricular approach. So how did they feel now in the secondary school, with subjects being separate?

> Everything now seems so plain compared to what we were doing in that project. Doing it you thought so much about everything you were doing, trying to put it into perspective and to think of it as real life and trying to make everyone else think about it. Now I am just doing school work and I don't feel as motivated nor want to do it as much. I could put what I actually felt about things into that project. Now I have to concentrate on every separate lesson.

When I do something in English then go to maths and I can't mix it all together like I might want to. I prefer it mixed into one because then you can really say your feelings but here you just have to get on with your work, answer the questions, and do what the teacher tells you.

It would be far more exciting learning as well if things were joined together because instead of just doing separate things you could work on things more together and do what we wanted to do some of the time. Things could be joined together but because we have separate lessons at separate times and we have to move around to other rooms – we can still bring it in our minds – but it is really difficult to settle down in a different atmosphere and then try to think about the same thing you were thinking about in the last lesson because you have to get on with what you have to do now.

Now you know what you have to do. You know you have to do maths and then English whereas in primary school you did do those lessons but you didn't do them in a set order and you did different things in different ways. It wasn't as if you were doing one subject after another in the same order week after week. It was different every day. In the primary school subjects that might seem opposite like English and maths we actually mixed the English with the maths.

These youngsters from Ipplepen are articulating both here and in their discussion in Chapter 5 some crucial aspects about learning that cross-curricular work positively encourages and promotes.

Creativity in learning

The talk of these young people here and in Chapter 5 indicates how each of them found an unique way of expressing what s/he knows and feels and how much of a sense of self-esteem and personal fulfilment that ability to be creative and express-ive has given them.

Linking school learning with the community

The production involved the children working with and for others. Many parents helped with costumes, set-building,

136

props and so on. A community artist taught the children how to make the masks used in the production. Parents, teachers, children, friends and relations went as a community together to the Barclay Awards in London. The children also became more aware of being part of the global community. They were touched by the lives, fears and ambitions of a people half-way across the world.

Making connections between subjects

The pupils clearly found links helpful. As the quote above so tellingly shows, the way these links were achieved in the primary school they attended gave them a sense of being in more control of their learning.

Knowledge is seen as being flexible and fascinating

The way the children talked about the development of their personal involvement in the project as they went deeper and deeper into the subject is recognition of the interrelationship between the affective and the cognitive aspects of the individual. In other words if we feel involved, if our emotions become engaged then we are stimulated to learn. We construct new meanings and understandings out of what we know already because it matters. The girl talking about the way she made her speech as a black person is a good example of this.

Valuing of different ways of knowing

Learning through the medium of the creative arts, aesthetic practical activities (movement, dance, drama and song) had equal status as a learning strategy alongside academic learning where the teacher transmitted new ideas and the children were involved in reading, writing, speaking and listening. This went hand in hand with art and design productive activities of mask-making and set construction – all integrated through the theme of racism in South Africa – propositional, practical and productive knowledge working together coherently.

137

This book has celebrated these aspects of learning and has argued the case for their proper inclusion in the school curriculum via the cross-curricular themes, dimensions and skills. Finally, in the spirit of an important dimension to this book, the inclusion of the thoughts, feelings and actions of a new generation of teachers, this book ends with a positive and uplifting comment from a student teacher. She is seeking to come to terms with understanding the coherent link between knowledge organized into separate subjects and cross-curricular work. It neatly sums up the principal underlying values that this book has sought to articulate about an across-the-curriculum approach to educating young people from 5 to 16.

When I first began to think about the cross-curriculum themes, dimensions and skills and their relationships to the subjects within the National Curriculum and to each other, I began to think at first of layers that combined to make the complete curriculum. Then I began to realize that this was rather two-dimensional. The curriculum was more like a sculpture that is only understood by looking at it from many different angles – the subjects being the basis and the themes and dimensions being the different perspectives to view it from. At this point it dawned on me that I had misunderstood completely. The curriculum does not belong to us as teachers. We do not own it nor do we stand outside it. We are participants in it. So then I though of being like a guide leading a guided tour but still this was not quite right. Then it hit me.

Knowledge is a mass, an amalgam that we attempt to rationalize to allow children to access it. What we forget is that children already know how to access it. It is we who have forgotten. So this led me to my analogy. The curriculum has to be viewed as a giant playground with orange slides and green tunnels and red things you can climb over and round and through. We have made children stop their natural curiosity and we have conducted them logically around the playground and they have found it boring! What cross-curricular themes could be is an opportunity for a new way to play in the playground where we rediscover our love of learning and children never lose theirs! If this is empowerment, then that is what it is about. All we should be as teachers are people who have been in the playground longer and we should be saying, 'Use the skills you have and try hanging upside down on those bars'. Cross-curricular dimensions then become taking your turn on the slide and not pushing anyone off the roundabout and the subjects are the structures through which, around which and on which the experience of activity can be explored. We have forgotten how to play. We have bowed to external pressures that tell us that play is an educational four-letter word. We are afraid to be seen to be less in control of classrooms and both we and the children have suffered.

(from an essay by Diane Summers, 1992)

REFERENCES

Baelz, P. R. (1980) Philosophy of health education, in Sutherland, I. (ed.) *Health Education Perspectives and Choices*. London: Allen & Unwin.

Bennett, N. (1990) The primary curriculum, in Brown, T. and Morrison, K. (eds), *The Curriculum Handbook*. London: Longman.

Black, P. (1992) Prejudice, tradition and death of a dream, shortened version of Professor Paul Black's address to the educational section of the British Association for the Advancement of Science, reported in *Times Educational Supplement*, 28 August.

Black, P. J. (1988) *The Task Group on Assessment and Testing*. Unpublished paper presented at one day BERA (British Educational Research Association) Conference on Benchmark Testing, 11 February.

Broadfoot, P. (1988), letter to the Nuffield Seminar Group.

Brown, S. (1990) Assessment: a changing practice, in Horton, T. (ed.) *Assessment Debates*, London: Hodder and Stoughton.

CBI (1989) *Towards a Skills Revolution*. London: Confederation of British Industry.

Clarke, K. (1992) *Education in a Classless Society*. Westminster Lecture to the Tory Reform Group, 12 June 1992.

Curtis, S. J. (1967) *History of Education in Great Britain*, London: University Tutorial Press.

Dearing, R. (1993) *The National Curriculum and Its Assessment: An Interim Report*. National Curriculum Council/Schools Examinations and Assessment Council.

DES (1967) Report of the Central Advisory Council for Education (England) *Children and Their Primary Schools* (Plowden Report). London: HMSO.

DES (1985) *Better Schools*. London: HMSO.

DES (1986) *Health Education from 5 to 16: Curriculum Matters 6*. London: HMSO.

DES/DoE (1987) *Working Together for a Better Future*. London: DES/DoE.

DES (1988) *Careers Education and Guidance from 5–16: Curriculum Matters 10*. London: HMSO.

Devlin, T. and Warnock, M. (1977) *What Must We Teach?* London: Temple Smith.

Dewey, J. (1966) *Democracy and Education*. New York: The Free Press.

Eraut, M., Pennycuick, D. and Radnor, H. (1987) *Local Evaluation of INSET, a Meta-evaluation of TRIST Evaluations*. Bristol: NCD/SMT.

Frederikson, J. and Collins, A. (1989) A systems approach to educational testing, *Educational Researcher*, **18** (9), 27–32.

Goodson, I. (1983) *School Subjects and Curriculum Change*. London: Croom Helm.

Hamilton, D. (1990) *Learning about Education: An Unfinished Curriculum*. Milton Keynes: Open University Press.

Hargreaves, D. (1982) *The Challenge for the Comprehensive School*. London: Routledge and Kegan Paul.

Hargreaves, D. (1991) Coherence and manageability: reflections on the National Curriculum and cross-curricular provision, *Curriculum Journal*, **2** (1), 32–41.

Hirst, P. (1969) The logic of the curriculum, *Journal of Curriculum Studies*, **1** (2), 142–58.

Horner, (1980) Health education and public policy in the United Kingdom, *Community Medicine*, **2** (3), 229–35.

Jamieson, I. (1991) School work and real work: economic and industrial understanding in the curriculum, *Curriculum Journal*, **2** (1), 55–67.

Jenkins and Shipman (1976) *Curriculum: An Introduction*. London: Open Books.

Kogan, M. (1978) *The Politics of Educational Change*. London: Methuen.

Nixon, J. (1981) *A Teacher's Guide to Action Research*. London: McIntyre Grant.

Paris, S., Lawton, T. A. Turner, J. C. and Roth, J. L. (1991) A developmental perspective on standardized achievement testing, *Educational Researcher*, **20** (5), 12–20.

Phenix, P. (1962) The uses of the disciplines as curriculum content, *Educational Forum* **26**, 273–80.

Pring, R. (1987) The curriculum and the new vocationalism, *British Journal of Education and Work*, **3** 133–48.

Pring, R. (1992) *Changes in Curriculum and Assessment*, unpublished paper.

Relph, E. (1982) *Place and Placelessness*. London: Pion.

Roach, J. (1971) *Public Examinations in England 1850–1900*. Cambridge: CUP.

Rowe, G. and Whitty, G. (1993) Five themes remain in shadows *TES* 9 April 1993.

SCDC (1988) *Understand the Law: Law in Education Project*. London: Edward Arnold.

Smith, F. (1931) *A History of English Elementary Education 1760–1902*. London: University of London Press.

Speaker's Commission (1990) *Encouraging Citizenship*, Report of the Commission on Citizenship. London: HMSO.

Stenhouse, L. (1975) *Introduction to Curriculum Research and Development*. Oxford: Heinemann Educational.

Sutherland, I. (ed.) (1980) *Health Education: Perspectives and Choices*. London: Allen & Unwin.

TGAT (1988) *National Curriculum Task Group on Assessment and Testing: A Report*. London: DES and the Welsh Office.

The National Curriculum Council (1990a) *Curriculum Guidance 3: The Whole Curriculum*. York: NCC.

The National Curriculum Council (1990b) *Curriculum Guidance 4: Education for Economic and Industrial Understanding*. York: NCC.

The National Curriculum Council (1990c) *Curriculum Guidance 5: Health Education*. York: NCC.

The National Curriculum Council (1990d) *Curriculum Guidance 6: Careers Education and Guidance*. York: NCC.

The National Curriculum Council (1990e) *Curriculum Guidance 7: Environmental Education*. York: NCC.

The National Curriculum Council (1990f) *Curriculum Guidance 8: Education for Citizenship*. York: NCC.

Torrance, H. (1989) Theory, practice and politics in the development of assessment, *Cambridge Journal of Education*, **19** (2), 183–91.

Tyler, R. (1986) Changing concepts of educational evaluation, *International Journal of Educational Research*, **10** (1).

Weston, P. (1992) A decade of differentiation, *British Journal of Special Education*, **19** (1), 6–9.

Whitty, G. (1985) *Sociology and School Knowledge*. London: Methuen.

WHO (World Health Organization) (1978) *Primary Health Care*. A report of the International Conference on Primary Health Care.

Williams, R. (1961) *The Long Revolution*. Harmondsworth: Penguin.

Wolf, D. (1988) Opening up assessment, *Educational Leadership*, **45** (4), 24–9.

Wood, R. (1987) *Measurement and Assessment in Education and Psychology*. Lewes: Falmer Press.

Wragg, T. (1993) The fire is out but who will clear up the mess? *Observer*, 8 August 1993.

Index